A Special Gift

Also by Carolyn Faulder

WHOSE BODY IS IT?
THE WOMAN'S CANCER BOOK
* *

With Ruth Mankel
MOVING UP
* *

With Paul Brown
TREAT YOURSELF TO SEX

A Special Gift

The Story of Dr Vicky Clement-Jones and
the foundation of BACUP

Carolyn Faulder

Michael Joseph
LONDON

MICHAEL JOSEPH LTD

Published by the Penguin Group
27 Wrights Lane, London W8 5TZ, England
Viking Penguin Inc., 375 Hudson Street, New York, New York, 10014, USA
Penguin Books Australia Ltd, Ringwood, Victoria, Australia
Penguin Books Canada Ltd, 10 Alcorn Avenue, Toronto, Ontario, Canada M4V 3B2
Penguin Books (NZ) Ltd, 182–190 Wairau Road, Auckland 10, New Zealand

Penguin Books Ltd, Registered Offices: Harmondsworth, Middlesex, England

First published in Great Britain 1991

Copyright © Carolyn Faulder

Printed in England by Clays Ltd, St Ives plc
Filmset in Monophoto Palatino 12/14

A CIP catalogue record for this book is available from the British Library
ISBN 0 7181 3442 7

The moral right of the author has been asserted

Sweet are the uses of adversity,
Which, like the toad, ugly and venomous
Wears yet a precious jewel in his head;
And this our life, exempt from public haunt,
Finds tongues in trees, books in the running brooks,
Sermons in stones, and good in everything.

(William Shakespeare,
As You Like It II.i.12)

Contents

❖

Preface

❖

B ACUP stands for the British Association of Cancer United Patients. It is a charity which was founded in 1985 by Dr Vicky Clement-Jones, following her own experience of ovarian cancer. It offers information, practical help, advice and emotional support to cancer patients and their families and friends.

The services it provides include:

– a telephone Cancer Information Service run by trained cancer nurses who will also answer written requests for information

– a Cancer Counselling Service

– a range of publications on the main types of cancer, their treatments, and different ways of living and coping with cancer

– a newspaper, *BACUP News* which is published three times a year.

All these services are provided free of charge. BACUP depends entirely on voluntary contributions.

Vicky Clement-Jones believed that 'knowledge is the antidote to fear'. Her own short and remarkable life bore this out. This is her story and the story of the charity she founded.

Foreword

❖

I ONLY MET Vicky Clement-Jones once, sometime in 1986. I had been introduced to BACUP by Mr Peter Wrigley and went along one morning to 'meet the staff', as it were, of this new-found help line which dealt with the even then almost unmentionable disease of cancer. For some strange reason the word was avoided in conversation whenever possible. People were spoken of as having 'something nasty' or, perhaps more daringly, as having 'the big C'. The word cancer was hardly ever used. It terrified people and it was hidden under euphemistic names. No one wanted to discuss this large and indeed frightening problem. The subject was, to all intents and purposes, taboo. Someone very close to me was gravely ill with the disease; Peter Wrigley was the doctor in charge, and through him I got to learn more about cancer than I had ever thought possible.

Sensing my interest and desire to assist in whatever way I could any charity which dealt with the problem, he invited me to meet Dr Vicky Clement-Jones. When we met I was unaware she herself was a victim of the disease and more to the point that she had only, a few moments before, left her sick bed in order to welcome me and, as I very soon realized, to 'grab' me as someone who might possibly help her in her efforts to raise money for her project.

She was, as all of us who had the good fortune to know her, even slightly as I did, a very determined creature. Without this determination, she could not have fought her wretched illness so triumphantly for longer than it was ever expected that she would. Nor could she have devised and created BACUP.

She was aware from the moment that she knew she had the disease that others could be placed in her situation; that there were indeed a great many anxious, frightened, bewildered families who were having to 'come to terms' with this illness which carried the terrible stigma of fatality. She knew that courage, counsel and support were essential. No one had thought of helping cancer victims and their families and friends in this way before.

Vicky Clement-Jones vowed to cope with her own distress in a positive and helpful way. If she were to die she would at least help those in pain; fight and work for the people who most needed care and love; and give advice and organize help for those in despair. The life which she had to endure was borne with exceptional courage, helped by the awareness that she was not alone. Her example provided inspiration and steadfast help for many. There were thousands of people out in the darkness of ignorance who had found just what she had. People were not equipped to cope with the suddenness of cancer. Families were uncertain, afraid and bewildered. Even family doctors, to whom one naturally turned for help, were unable or unwilling to do so, or simply uncertain in their explanations.

So Vicky Clement-Jones decided to start BACUP. To help sufferers and their families who found themselves exactly where she had found herself. Adrift. Unsure. Frightened. In need of advice.

BACUP supplies that need abundantly.

On the day that we met in Charterhouse Street, I joined Vicky Clement-Jones with fellow doctors at a busy, crowded table amid a thriving atmosphere of friendship, noise, beer, sausages and mash. I did not know, nor was I told, that the tiny (for she was indeed sparrow-like) creature sitting among us, vibrant, eager, full of ideas for this amazing charity into which she had invited me was, in fact, dying. At the end of our luncheon she went back to her hospital, and her bed. The effort had cost her; but she was not going to allow that to interfere with anything.

This, then, is the story of an exceptional woman; a woman of great courage and indeed vision, who, facing almost certain death, fought back and thought of the people she might now be able to help. She was as ruthless with herself as she was with anything to do with her dream of BACUP. It succeeded ultimately in becoming a highly successful enterprise: from a staggering walk it moved into a steady canter, and when she finally died she knew that it was a lusty child. It would survive; and survive it has, to honour the memory of an incredibly brave and determined woman.

We who knew her, even marginally as I did, are the stronger for our knowledge of her. She was proof to us all that if obstacles get in the way of what you feel you must do, they simply have to be overcome. Simple if you have the guts: Vicky Clement-Jones had courage, and time to spare for everyone.

DIRK BOGARDE

Capsize

❖

IN AUGUST 1982 Dr Vicky Clement-Jones was thirty-three. A string of academic successes marked her progress and a glittering future in the medical world lay before her. She was a senior registrar and held a clinical research fellowship in the department of endocrinology at St Bartholomew's Hospital in the City of London. Already her name was beginning to attract attention in the higher reaches of endocrinology and its related disciplines and she had been invited to give papers at several international conferences. Her career beckoned enticingly and although she felt she was shortly approaching a crossroads where she might have to decide between academic or clinical medicine she was champing to confront the challenge. There was her thesis to complete for her MD and then, who knows what appointment might not be offered to her? There was also the private excitement of preparing for the children that she and her husband Tim were now eager to have after nine years of marriage.

Vicky was glad all the same that this particular summer was fading and coming to an end. For it had been the most fraught time she could ever remember. She seemed to have staggered from crisis to crisis.

There had been two serious illnesses: the first, in early 1981, a severe bout of rheumatic fever which was followed some six months later by a perforated appendix resulting in peritonitis and the discovery of a pelvic abscess. Both had entailed dramatic dashes to hospital followed by periods of long, tedious convalescence which, for one normally so healthy and always abnormally energetic, had been hard to bear.

There had been frustrations in her working life as well, most recently the disappointment of not being offered a coveted promotion for which she was well qualified and had been certain would be hers. Even her ebullient husband, Tim, who was as dedicated a politician as Vicky was a doctor, was not, it seemed, to be spared the jinx. The Liberal party, of which he was a leading light, had failed to win a single seat in Streatham, where he had worked so hard, in the local council elections in May.

'A trail of minor defeats' is the typically laconic way she described their recent setbacks in a letter to her close friend, Alison, then living in the States. It was none the less heartfelt and the nearest Vicky would allow herself to complain, but she was tired, physically and emotionally. For too long she felt she had been sailing through choppy seas, striving to keep her small craft upright and afloat. Now she was exhausted and longing to find a quiet haven where she could rest a while and recover her strength before embarking with renewed vigour on the next stage of her career.

The one highlight of the year had been their trip in February to the Far East and Australia to visit relatives from which she had returned feeling exhilarated but, as spring changed to summer, her vitality began to wane again and the abdominal pains and bowel problems of the previous year returned. She feared a flare-up of the pelvic abscess and in July returned to hospital for tests which included a barium enema. The doctors examining her shared her suspicions but said she need not cancel the short trip to Hawaii to celebrate her father's seventieth birthday which had been booked months earlier. They would continue their examinations when she returned.

Her swashbuckling millionaire father, Teddy Yip, enjoyed nothing better than throwing lavish parties for his friends and large Chinese family. His birthday provided an annual excuse for an extra special entertainment and this year was to be no exception. At the end of July Vicky and Tim flew out to Honolulu where they joined her mother Susie, her brothers George and Ronnie, and her sisters Tina and Betty, together with their assorted spouses, children and a few old friends. They celebrated their father's birthday at a big dinner and, as always, it was a noisy, emotionally charged occasion. This time feelings ran even higher than usual when Teddy announced he had once again become a father in May of that year.

Vicky's miniscule diary for this period records in dispassionate note form her physical state — mucous, diarrhoea and bleeding every day — but, quite typically, makes no reference to her feelings. However, she, like her sister Tina and the other members of the family, but especially her mother Susie, had been very upset by her father's disclosure. Although he had never made any secret of his womanizing, the announcement of this unexpected addition to their family was disturbing.

On their way back to England, Vicky and Tim had passed through the States, stopping off to see friends, including Alison and her husband Michael. Both of them doctors, Michael Farthing was enjoying a two-year assignment as visiting associate professor at a medical school in Cambridge, Massachusetts, while Alison had a fellowship in radiology at a nearby hospital.

Alison was heavily pregnant with her first child and the two women, close friends from Cambridge days, had much to catch up on and news to exchange. However, the Farthings had observed with some concern that Vicky was uncharacteristically subdued. After a day's outing Michael had been moved to do something rather unusual. He had assumed his professional role as a gastroenterologist and examined

Vicky on the sitting-room floor. He felt a mass in her stomach and wondered to himself whether it could be due to Crohn's disease, a chronic inflammation of the small intestine, which might account for the colicky pains and other symptoms she was experiencing. He did not say anything to Vicky but certainly it never occurred to him that it could be anything else of a more sinister nature.

Vicky returned to England on 8th August feeling shattered and drained. At once she started to have more tests at St Bartholomew's Hospital, or Barts as it is familiarly called by doctors, patients, and every Londoner. She had an ultra sound and finally a CT scan, a special type of X-ray which feeds a series of pictures into a computer and builds up a detailed view of the inside of the body. It was the scan which revealed the mass which Michael had felt earlier.

Professor Taylor, the surgeon, decided to perform an abdominal operation (laparatomy) to investigate what he and everyone else were now convinced must be a return of the pelvic abscess.

'Well, this has all been rather a blow,' Vicky wrote to Alison, five days after her operation. She had been diagnosed with cancer of the ovaries, inoperable because it was at an advanced stage. The doctors gave her three months to live. She expected to be dead by Christmas.

Tim had taken Vicky into Barts on 18th August and the operation was scheduled to take place the following day at three in the afternoon. She was last on the operating list which is usual practice where infection is suspected because of the pus which would be present in the abscess and could contaminate the theatre for other cases. Vicky, as was her wont, occupied her time usefully by helping the houseman to put up the drips for other patients. As the time approached for her pre-med she felt a trifle uneasy. She couldn't help wondering what they would find, but the timing of the operation reassured her.

She awoke later that evening feeling very groggy from the anaesthetic to find the houseman, a young Chinese doctor from Hong Kong, standing by her bedside.

'Was it an abscess?' she asked him immediately.

'No,' he stuttered. 'It wasn't an abscess. They've taken a biopsy and the professor will come and see you tomorrow.'

Oh, my goodness, thought Vicky to herself. Something's up. It must be serious if they are taking a biopsy, but why aren't they telling me? Still in a haze she consoled herself with the thought that maybe she was having a bad dream and that if she went back to sleep it would go away.

But when she woke up in the morning the dream became dreadful reality. The senior registrar was the first to visit her. He shuffled uncomfortably, pulling the curtains round her bed to give her some privacy. His expression was gloomy. Avoiding the mention of words like 'tumour' or 'malignancy' he told her that the surgeon had discovered a mass in her pelvis and had decided to take a biopsy. Shortly afterwards, she was visited by Professor Taylor, her surgeon, and Mr Shepherd, a younger surgeon who was making a name for himself in the treatment of female cancers; he had been called into the theatre during her operation to give an opinion.

Cancer, Vicky noticed, was a word everyone had difficulty saying but the doctors were trying hard to be honest. They told her that they thought it was ovarian but they were unwilling to commit themselves to a definite opinion about its exact nature and stage until the pathologist had analysed the biopsied tissue. It was clear, though, to everyone that it was an advanced cancer since other organs in the pelvic cavity as well as her ovaries had been infiltrated. She was keenly aware of their pessimism and that people were looking away from her, trying not to meet the questions in her eyes. The buzz had gone round the hospital grapevine. Everyone knew that Vicky, the brilliant young doctor, was gravely ill with cancer.

'I think the worse thing of all is not knowing,' she wrote in that same letter to Alison, 'and then knowing other people's reaction to it. I felt so sorry for Prof. Taylor, the SR [Senior Registrar] and the HP [House Physician] who somehow felt they were responsible!'

After the doctors, Tim came. Again the curtains were pulled round her bed and Vicky told him the bad news. They cried together and then, with that capacity to see a 'silver lining' in every disaster, a quality they shared in abundance, they resolved they would make the best of whatever time was left to them. They told each other how lucky they had been.

'You can't say T. and I haven't had a run for our money,' she continued her letter to Alison. 'We've had fun now for some 14 years! – yes – we really have been together that long.' Some years later she was to expand that sentiment in her radio interview with the psychiatrist Professor Anthony Clare to whom she said: 'The happiness we've had together some people don't have in a whole lifetime.'

She also kept her sense of humour, observing to Alison that 'Tim's taken it very well and it has been an impetus to him to get all those jobs done round the house that I have been nagging about for months – I'm pleased to say!'

Vicky had been told that there was really very little the doctors could do for her. Her operation was followed by, as she admitted, a few 'really horrific' days of injections, drips, catheters, another CT scan and so on. Yet, after all this she could finish her letter, urging Alison not to worry about her because, now that all that was behind her, she was going to think positively, wait for what treatment lay ahead, get better, and definitely finish her thesis.

This was not false heroics as anyone who knew Vicky at all

well could testify. She meant it and she was determined to achieve her goals; that was the way she always reacted to problems. So her response was totally genuine, even though with the other side of her mind she had accepted that her life expectancy had been reduced to three months. Later she was to say on many occasions how 'lucky' she had been to have the two previous illnesses because they enabled her and those closest to her to cope so much better when the big one — cancer — came along.

All the same, a sense of profound anguish prevailed in those dark days after the diagnosis while they were waiting for the biopsy results to come through. She described them poignantly in an article she wrote for the *British Medical Journal* as 'Four days of devastation, fear, anger, and the question "why me?" . . . The sadness and numbness of the diagnosis shattered my world and the horizons and expectations that my husband and I had known . . . I was left with the thought that no treatment was available.'

One of the ways of reducing her sense of helplessness was to talk about what was going on. Tim sprang into action and telephoned around the world to both families and all their friends. It was deliberately done, all part of the plan he and Vicky had already made that they intended to be totally frank about her illness. They wanted neither to keep secrets nor hear whispers. Vicky was often to say how grateful she had been to Tim for taking this burden of explanation from her. It meant that everyone knew where they were with her and could talk openly to her about what was going on. Tim gave them the facts, all that he and Vicky knew at that stage, and warned them that they would be depending on their support and love in the coming months. David Poole, a very dear friend of theirs, cut short his holiday to be at Vicky's bedside on Saturday, just two days after her operation. Betty, Vicky's younger sister, walked in unexpectedly at two o'clock on that same Saturday afternoon.

On Sunday, her father, an inveterate globe-trotter, happened to arrive in London and came at once to see her. Much later Vicky recalled how grateful she was to him for being so unexpectedly considerate and understanding. 'He was the only one who had hope for me and he told me I had to keep fighting. I really took that to heart.'

On Monday her mother stepped off the plane from Australia looking 'absolutely fresh, crisp and blooming' according to her admiring daughter and immediately cooked her a Chinese dinner. Some of her hospital colleagues popped in at odd moments during the day and regaled her with gossipy stories, which encouraged her to think she might soon be back working beside them.

Her reunion with David was especially emotional. They had been close friends ever since they met in 1974 when she had been a novice doctor doing her first house job at Lambeth Hospital where he was a registrar. But it was the interests they shared outside their medical working lives which really brought them together. Music, in particular, was a great passion for both of them and they had been playing duets together for many years on a regular basis. Vicky was an accomplished pianist who had even toyed at one time with the idea of becoming a professional musician. David was not so technically competent but he had an instinct and feeling for music which made him a very good accompanist.

It was natural now for Vicky to seek David's advice and confide in him about the way she intended to handle her cancer. She had determined from the outset to be positive and she shuddered at the thought that she might in some way exploit her illness as a form of emotional blackmail. She and David remembered with great sadness a friend of theirs from the St Thomas days who had done just that. According to Vicky, she had virtually stage-managed her announcement of her breast cancer to a group of selected friends at the end of a good evening together and left them all feeling very guilty that they were cancer-free while she was doomed to die. Bitter and angry at the blow that had been dealt her, this unhappy woman was determined everyone should suffer with her and, as she began, so she continued until indeed she did die. It was a divisive and unhappy time for everyone who knew her.

Her behaviour and the effect it had had on David, who had known her much better than Vicky did, made such a deep impression on her nonetheless, that when it was her turn to deal with the unthinkable, it was this woman's face which kept coming out of the shadows towards her. Not like her, Vicky vowed. I will not be like her.

So here she was, feeling sick and wretched with her cancer, no future to speak of, just waiting to hear what the doctors thought they might be able to do for her. Her little craft had been well and truly capsized by a monster wave. All she could do was hang on and try to hope.

'It was rather like being lost off a boat in a storm and thinking there was no further hope because you were just clinging on to a piece of wood,' she was later to tell the psychiatrist Anthony Clare.

Battered and bruised she may have been but she was not yet defeated. Vicky felt wonderfully supported and cherished by those she loved most in the world. She could not guess what was waiting for her out there on that stormy sea but whatever the fates brought her, she was determined she would fight hard to survive.

But to understand how she became such a fighter, we must go back to her early years.

2

Spare Baggage

❖

(1948–1954)

VICKY VERONICA YIP was a Christmas baby. The third child of Teddy and Susie Yip, she was born in the French Hospital in Hong Kong on 23rd December 1948, where she was delivered by a nun midwife because Susie could not afford to pay a doctor's fees. The baby's head was the size of an orange, according to her mother, and she remembers Vicky's birth as the easiest of her five children.

The new-born Vicky spent her first Christmas in hospital with her mother who shared a ward with three other women. As soon as Susie felt strong enough she took the baby home to her cramped flat where the two older children, Tina aged three and George fifteen months old, were waiting for them. Situated in the heart of the Shau Kei Wan district which is near the ferry and was then, as now, a rundown district, the converted ground-floor shop was not an ideal home for a growing family.

It consisted of one large room divided by a thin partition wall into a sitting room at the front and kitchen behind. The primitive lavatory in one corner at the back was the kind where you squat with your feet on either side of the hole. There was a cold water tap in the kitchen and they used a bucket for washing. Teddy and Susie had a small bedroom above on the mezzanine floor.

As a tiny baby, Vicky had digestive problems, seemingly

more than the usual colic. Susie worried that it was because she could not produce enough milk to satisfy the baby and the formula milk seemed to cause her a lot of wind and discomfort. Whatever the reason, in those early months Vicky cried ceaselessly. Tina remembers their nurse trying to soothe Vicky by laying a coin wrapped in tissue paper on her navel but all to no avail. The screaming infuriated her father so when he was at home Susie would snatch the baby up, wrap her in a shawl and put her in the tiny lavatory, trying to remove the source of irritation as far away as possible. Unappeased, he would threaten to flush the baby down the lavatory, a story Vicky would recount with considerable relish in later years. She enjoyed seeing her friends' shocked reaction.

Susie was not accustomed to living in such straitened circumstances but then her fortunes had changed dramatically since she had been swept off her feet by the dashing Teddy a few years earlier. Theirs had been a shipboard romance during the Second World War on the way to Saigon where she and her older sister, Winnie, reputed to be the most beautiful girl in South East Asia, had been sent by their father, Ho Sai Kwon. He feared with good reason that if his lovely daughters stayed any longer in Hong Kong the invading Japanese generals would take them as concubines. Ho Sai Kwon belonged to one of the richest and most influential families in Hong Kong. The original family name was Bossman which the Chinese had shortened to Ho. In the early nineteenth century it was quite usual for Europeans to take Chinese concubines and their children would then be taken into the family business. In the case of Susie's family this was the renowned Jardine, Matheson trading company where for several generations the Hos were employed as compradors. These were middlemen between the Western business community and the Chinese merchants. Their administrative skills, sharp eye for a good business opportunity and entrepreneurial talents soon turned them into wealthy tycoons in their own right. By the turn of the century Sir Robert Ho Tung, Susie's great-uncle, was a mega-millionaire.

When Teddy Yip, professional footballer and small-time businessman, met the eighteen-year-old Susie Ho, freshly released from her sheltered background, he was already in his early thirties, a seasoned man of the world, well known for his Casanova exploits and his wild partying and drinking. The son of an obscure customs official of mixed Chinese and Indonesian origins, he had been brought up in a small Indonesian village where he was educated by Dutch missionaries. He grew up speaking Dutch and English; the latter language, in particular, stood him in good stead when, as a young man, he started to cultivate the company of Europeans. Little is known about his early years but Susie, who knew her mother-in-law slightly, found her a fearsome woman who apparently used to tie the young Teddy to a table when he misbehaved and would leave him there all day. This unhappy upbringing may explain some of Teddy's later erratic behaviour towards his own family.

The marriage was stormy right from the beginning but in spite of her difficulties and lack of money Susie was glad to have a home of her own. For a while, when Teddy was looking for work in Bangkok, she had returned to her parents who lived in a large rambling house in a smarter quarter of Hong Kong but she had not enjoyed the experience.

Her mother, Flora Sin Hall, was of Eurasian stock like her husband but despite running a household with two kitchens, one English and one Chinese, she remained deeply rooted in the Chinese tradition. Strong-willed and narrow-minded, she ruled her husband and her large brood with a rod of iron. Her thirteen children were brought up to expect an English breakfast of tea and porridge every morning and, every afternoon, a typical English tea with scones, sandwiches and cakes, but there the resemblance to English life ended. Chinese families expect their daughters, once married, to be off their hands.

They become their husband's responsibility, so when Flora's favourite son Stanley announced his wife's pregnancy she decided that the married couple should be given a suite of rooms and she told Susie that she no longer had space for her and her daughter Tina. Susie returned to Saigon. However, no sooner did Teddy hear that Susie had borne him a son, George, than he returned immediately from Bangkok and asked Susie to join him once more in Hong Kong. Vicky was born a year later.

She arrived at a time when her father's finances were at their lowest ebb. Although he was an ace salesman he felt keenly that he lacked the capital and the contacts he needed to make the serious money he wanted. And now here was yet another mouth to feed! One, furthermore, which was female, always open and for ever bawling.

As a baby, Vicky, in the manner of many Chinese children, had a shock of straight black hair which stood on end as if she were in a permanent state of petrified electrocution. There is a Chinese superstition that money is easily brushed out of hair like this. For Teddy, a devoutly superstitious Roman Catholic who could always find room in his lexicon of beliefs to accommodate a new superstition, this was enough to convince him that he had a real loser in this second daughter of his. He needed no further persuading when, shortly after Vicky's birth, a business deal went badly wrong and he lost a lot of money. Now he knew for certain that this useless girl child was bringing him bad luck and he wanted nothing of her.

'Spare baggage' is a term used by the Chinese to mean daughter and describes with chilling clarity the indifference the Chinese so often feel about their girl children and the little worth they accord them. Vicky was too small to remember any of this antipathy directed towards her but she was told about it often enough as she grew up for it to become part of the family lore. Her sense of being unloved and unwanted was deepened by the attitude of their nurse who, in typical Chinese fashion, spoilt the boys and smacked the girls.

Vicky's earliest memories date from Burma where Teddy had moved his family in 1950. Ever a gambler, he had decided to stake his last thousand dollars on a slap-up reception in the Hong Kong hotel to which he invited a local boy made good who was on a home visit to Hong Kong from the United States of America. His guest was the son of an immensely rich man known to everyone as the Sugar King, whose Kian Gwan Company had estates throughout South East Asia. The bold gesture paid off, handsomely. Teddy was offered the manager-ship of the Sugar King's estates in Burma.

For Susie and her family the transfer proved to be a fairytale transformation from penury in Shau Kei Wan to luxury in Rangoon. It marked a major change for the better in the family fortunes. From now on they would never again be quite as poor; ultimately, they would be very rich.

In Burma everything was paid for on a grand scale: the house was spacious and comfortable; there were plenty of servants; Teddy earned a large salary and was given generous expenses to entertain visiting businessmen. Susie thrived on the social life and the lavish entertaining she was now able to do.

The first memory Vicky could record was of her younger brother Ronnie's birth in 1952. All the family were gathered together in the sitting room including her baby sister, Betty, who had been born the year before in Hong Kong when Susie had returned to be near her dying mother. The room was packed with servants and various other employees of her father who were always hovering close to him.

'I do not actually remember seeing my father there,' wrote Vicky many years later. 'I just remember the tension in the air due to his presence. He only needed to be in the house for us children and, actually everyone, to feel frightened ... His tension communicated to us like his every emotion.'

This baby was the only one Susie had at home with the luxury of a doctor and nurse in attendance. There was much bustle and noise upstairs. At last, when the excitement was becoming almost unbearable for the children constrained to wait in silence, Teddy entered. Vicky remembers 'an overjoyed expression on his face' as he announced the birth of their baby brother. The children broke loose and, in Vicky's words, 'rushed upstairs to see the new intruder to our household. He looked so small and insignificant to me, lying there so helpless, but he was to affect all our lives.'

The adult Vicky recalling that scene was also seeing from an adult perspective how that new son, 'the intruder', would displace her still further in her father's affection. Throughout her life Vicky believed that her birth had been a great disappointment to her parents. Before her came Tina and George — one of each sex so that was all right. After George they had both wanted another boy, to guarantee the succession so to speak. But along came Vicky instead and their reaction was to ignore her. After her came yet another girl but Betty had a very different character and she was soon to learn her own ways of attracting the attention she needed. And now here was Ronnie who need do no more than be himself. It was enough that he was a boy; one day he would be another man to carry on the family line and the family business. Teddy was beginning to develop a strong sense of dynasty. The Yips would be as good as the Hos. Of that he was determined but daughters had little part to play in his grand scheme except, of course, to be beautiful, well behaved and, in due course, bring him good sons-in-law.

Whether Vicky was as unloved as she believed herself to be in those early days is not so important as the effect her perception of her place in the family had on her character and her attitudes. It was to be lasting and profound. She could never shake off her sense of hurt and she could never stop proving herself, even when over and over again and in so many different spheres she had shown herself to be the top, the best, the brightest, and had received many public plaudits. So often in conversation with friends and acquaintances, or in the many interviews she would give towards the end of her life, she would return to those early, long-lost days when the little Vicky was striving so hard to make her parents, most especially her father, notice her; above all love her.

Teddy had frequent rows with his wife which, often as not, would end in violence. All the children remember seeing their mother being beaten and hit. Vicky recalled the anguish of being a helpless witness to her mother's pain and humiliation, combined with a sense of absolute terror that he might turn on one of them next.

'Life with father in the house was a perpetual nightmare,' she once wrote. Unpredictable, irascible, unreasonable, he subjected them all to his whims and fits of bad temper, picking on an individual child for no real reason. They could never guess in advance what might provoke his ire; it could be an ordinary everyday task which suddenly and inexplicably was being performed in a manner displeasing to him; or it could be because they had broken one of his 'iron rules' like forgetting to address him as 'Daddy' before speaking to him or forgetting to accept something from him in their right hand, the left hand meanwhile being kept firmly behind their back.

Whatever Teddy's rationalizations may have been, Vicky felt that she was at the mercy of a dangerous and illogical being. 'An elemental force' is one description of Teddy by someone who was in a position to know him well. 'A total enigma' is the view of George Haynes, an old family friend who often stayed with the Yips when they were living in Burma. He remembers very early on being impressed by Vicky's quite remarkable self-possession. On one particular occasion when Susie was not there, he recalled Vicky at the head of the table, directing him to sit on her right with the brothers and sisters ranged on either side. Vicky was clearly in charge, not only of the family but the servants as well who obeyed her orders without protest.

'How would you like your coffee, Uncle George?' the five year-old asked him, in faultless English. 'Is your room comfortable? Have you got all you need? Are the servants looking after you properly?' He found himself responding quite naturally as if to an adult, indeed as if it were her mother, Susie, sitting there.

'Vicky,' he said, 'was the perfect hostess, the perfect lady, like she was all her life.' He returned to his wife extolling 'this most extraordinary child' he had met. What struck him most forcibly about Vicky at that age was that there was absolutely no element of play-acting in her behaviour, no conscious seeking of attention. She was simply behaving in the way she knew her mother would expect her to treat an honoured guest. He found such cool command of a situation in one so young both engaging and amazing. As he watched her grow up he saw her develop this ability to take charge to a remarkable degree: whatever was happening, Vicky was always in control of herself and of the situation.

Vicky, possessed as she was of a strong instinct for survival, understood in the inchoate way of a young but extremely intelligent child that probably her only hope for getting through her childhood relatively unscathed was to keep her distance from her father. Physically, this was obviously essential, if only to avoid his flailing hands, but mentally and emotionally too, since self-revelation, anything that smacked of vulnerability would lay her open to his taunts and anger.

In later life Vicky recognized that this need to defend herself from her father's violent and unpredictable behaviour had developed in her a protective carapace against the world in general. She always found it difficult to participate in a group as just another member and on equal terms, as opposed to leading it; this was particularly the case where her involvement required some kind of lowering of barriers. Her emotional reserve was a quality many people remarked in her; even those who were closest to her and shared many intimate thoughts and moments with her recognized that beneath the exuberance and enthusiasm there was another Vicky who found it difficult to give all of herself away. It is quite possible that this element of withdrawal in her personality would always have existed, whatever might have been her relationship with her father, but there is no doubt that her childhood fear of Teddy never really left her and marked her indelibly, as it did her siblings, in different ways.

3

The Sandwich-Squeeze Child

❖

(1954–1957)

TEDDY TOOK HIS family back to Hong Kong in 1954, shortly before Ne Win drew down the bamboo curtain and imposed his uniquely oppressive brand of socialist dictatorship on Burma. After a short period in a two-storey house in Lyttleton Road they moved up to the Midlevel district just above the downtown commercial and shopping areas of Central and Queen's Road. Here they occupied a raised ground-floor flat in what was then called Lower Castle Road (now called simply Castle Road, but otherwise not much altered from the way it was in the early Fifties).

The building, a grey concrete block on the top corner of the steeply sloping road, is bleakly genteel. No lines of washing here, nor bustling street stalls to break up the unadorned façades; only the ubiquitous air-conditioning boxes clamped to the walls like dislocated television sets and flaking fly posters flapping at eye level to provide a momentary distraction for the occasional passer by.

Number 2B, the Yip flat, has a stern aspect. The windows framed in red-painted steel are shuttered by heavy interior grilles. The entrance is securely guarded today, as it was then, by a door of solid concertina steel which is kept pulled firmly across and locked.

It was here that the Yip children would return from school every afternoon. First there was homework to do and then their Chinese teacher would arrive to continue the lessons in reading and writing Mandarin which they had started in Burma. Their first language had always been English. In Burma they had gone to an English school. Now here in Hong Kong they were one of only two Eurasian families admitted to the exclusive Peak School in Plunkett Road on the Peak.

It was, and is, a typical English prep school for children up to thirteen, preparing them for the Common Entrance exam and public school back home. Run on the traditional lines beloved by expatriates the world over, the day would start with morning assembly. The pupils were segregated into four houses and there was a punctiliously applied system of awarding merit marks. Every day Tina, George and Vicky, dressed in the school uniform of white shirts and grey flannel skirts or shorts, would be accompanied by Chun, their nurse, to the Peak tram. A swift ride up one of the most spectacular funicular railways in the world and then a ten-minute uphill walk to the school.

Later, when there was more money and Teddy could afford a chauffeur to drive them to and from school, they would be allowed to stop and work off their high spirits playing games, either in the garden of their Aunt Priscilla's house or – their favourite place – in a special rocky recess on the road below the school which they made their own for a glorious half hour. The driver would park the car, give them something to eat while they changed out of their uniforms into dungarees and sweaters and then they could let their imaginations run riot.

Always erratic in his comings and goings, the children dreaded that their father would arrive before they went to bed because, if he did, inevitably the same scene would be enacted. Teddy would enquire of Susie and Chun whether there had been any transgressions. There was usually some minor misdemeanour to report, whereupon they would all be stood in a row in a corner of the room and Teddy would spank them vigorously with a long orange shoehorn. Sometimes, he would order them to administer their own punishment by exhorting them to smack themselves on the face. 'Harder, harder, harder,' he would urge them on, presumably on the sound Catholic principle that a spot of self-flagellation is worth any number of imposed mortifications.

By now Vicky was carving out her own special niche in the family. As the middle child and the one who temperamentally was much quieter and less assertive than the others, she was nonetheless determined that she was not going to be ignored. Having worked out for herself that what she really wanted above all else was to win the love and appreciation of her family, but most especially she wanted her father's admiration, she decided there was only one way to achieve the recognition she craved. She would be good, the best at everything she attempted — lessons, games, playing the piano, which she started learning at the age of eight, and anything else that presented a challenge to her. Her behaviour too would be exemplary and indeed, everyone who knew her as a child remembers her as obedient and unselfish. Vicky was determined to excel because she saw this as the only way she could attract and hold the attention for which she longed. Success would make her popular; it would also reassure her that she was every bit as good as her more favoured siblings.

The 'sandwich-squeeze child', as she was so often to describe herself in later life, the one pressed between older and younger brothers and sisters, each apparently with a stronger claim than her for parental notice and affection, had what she described as her 'first taste of the sweets of victory' when she won a prize from her father for a painting of a shipwreck. She depicted it in careful detail, lying on the ocean bed surrounded by fishes and vegetation. She had been determined to win so it was wonderful to become the centre of attention and hear everyone's praise. However, what counted most of all for Vicky was that she had won her father's approval.

Vicky thrived on challenge. She also feared failure as she would often admit with disarming candour. However, as is so often true of high achievers, she needed that fear to spur her on to ever greater heights. Each subsequent victory in her life would taste the sweeter just because it signified that once again she had banished the shadow of defeat. All during the years of growing up Vicky was possessed by a fundamental sense of inferiority. Was she clever? Was she good? Was she lovable? How could she know since no one seemed willing to tell her she was? At first she felt this complex keenly in relation to her brothers and sisters; later on it would be towards her school mates and then her fellow undergraduates. Her self-confidence only started to blossom towards the end of her university career when prizes and recognition were heaped upon her.

It was quite easy for Vicky to be well behaved. She had little difficulty in doing as she was told, getting on with her homework, keeping her things tidy; to her this kind of behaviour made sense. Quite apart from winning her the approval she was always seeking it also fitted in very well with a philosophy of life that she was beginning to develop, albeit unconsciously; namely, that there were important things to be done and the only way you could achieve them was by cutting down on the trivial and the time-wasting. She was later to write that she could not honestly say that as children they were ever taught about right and wrong in a moral sense although the practice of their Roman Catholic religion, inherited from Teddy, featured quite prominently in their upbringing. All they knew for certain in a rather uncertain world was that their father's moods were highly volatile and that when provoked his anger could be terrifying. Vicky realized that 'goodness' meant not offending him in any way, not even giving him the opportunity to suspect misbehaviour. But then she was able to observe that naughtiness and rebellious behaviour not only got you into trouble; it invariably meant that as part of the punishment you would be prevented from doing what you really wanted to do.

Vicky decided to make a virtue of being the useful member of the family. She enjoyed looking after the younger ones and keeping them amused but she thought of them more as charges in her care for whom she was responsible than as equals. The ones she wished to play with and be accepted by were the two older ones, Tina and George. After her father, George was then the most important person in Vicky's life, and so he was to remain throughout her childhood and into early adulthood. He meant many different things to her at many times, and all of them had a profound effect on her own character and development. Older than her by a scant year, he was the one she found it natural to look up to and emulate, all the more so because George embodied many of the positive qualities she regretted were lacking in her father.

George was cool, reliable and reasonable. He might get angry or upset but he would not demean himself by allowing others to see how much he cared. George was very clever and everyone was pleased with him for that because he was a boy and it would help him in his future career. Vicky admired his intelligence because she too was intelligent but no one commended her for that. Girls were not expected to be clever. Good, pretty and docile: yes, that was important because these were attributes that would help them make an advantageous marriage in due course. As it happened, Vicky was all of those things but what she prized above all was doing well at her lessons. She loved learning and she particularly enjoyed learning from George. He was the one who introduced her to books and ideas and interesting information about the world outside their closed family circle. Since there was little in the way of cultural influences coming from their parents she looked to George as her fount of wisdom. 'I wanted his wisdom to flow to me and reinforce what I felt was an inadequate personality,' she wrote as a nineteen-year-old.

George was her model and her rival, her father figure and even, in some respects, her enemy just because of who he was. His age, his gender and his ability were always there ahead of her, blocking, it seemed, her own endeavours and minimizing her successes. It became immensely important for Vicky in later years to prove not merely that she was as good as George but that she was better.

For now she just wanted to be as like him as possible. He was a boy so she would be boyish too. A natural tomboy, Vicky was never happier than when wearing boys' clothes and devising some game where almost invariably she would be the leader taking her valiant band into battle. She might die, but she would die with honour defending a just cause. Many years later Vicky wrote with endearing candour of her youthful self that she had found that 'being a martyr was one of the best ways of drawing attention to myself modestly'. Although she enjoyed playing boys' games and strove hard to identify with the opposite sex because she felt obscurely that this would put her in a more favourable light with her parents, she also remembered feeling resentful that they didn't somehow resist this tendency in her. 'Innately I felt it was all wrong.' Here again is the 'sandwich-squeeze child' voicing her sense of rejection.

She felt bitter, for instance, that she was never given her own doll to play with. Indeed, the only thing she could remember being entirely hers as a very small child was a teddy bear which went everywhere with her. All the other toys and games came out of the communal chest. This enforced sharing of possessions as a child in a large family made her value all the more the things she acquired in later life. She was always remarkably generous but she made no bones about the upset it caused her if a member of the family misused or broke something that belonged to her. She did not mind so much if the damage was caused by outsiders but the carelessness of a brother or sister would immediately reactivate the old resentment. They had had more than her when she was little. Why could they not respect her property now?

Vicky may not have been given dolls but she was given something else when she was seven years old which was to make a lasting impression on her. In the Chinese fashion her parents had decided that they would have a lawyer and a doctor in the family. George was destined for the first career. Vicky, so bright and so keen to be like her brother, would be the doctor, a profession regarded as acceptable for Chinese women. Susie remembers giving Vicky a doctor's set which Vicky loved from the first day. She knew exactly what to do with it: donning the white coat; fixing the stethoscope on Betty or Ronnie; asking them what their symptoms were and prescribing them a medicine. She soon decided that it could do with some improvement. Asking people how they felt was not good enough; they were too vague in their answers or they forgot things. She resolved that one day she would invent a machine which would read off their symptoms precisely and completely so that she could then have all the information she needed to make an accurate diagnosis and work out the treatment they needed.

Vicky often spoke of the doctor's set and the influence it had had on her life. From an early age she was thirsting for information, as much of it as she could absorb. As she grew older she realized that knowledge opens doors and that if you can communicate effectively what you know, then you can offer the key of change and improvement to others as well as yourself. The future clinician, the scientist, the dedicated researcher, and ultimately the founder of BACUP are all implicit in that seven-year-old's determination to discover more than just the facts about people; she wanted to understand them and help them by doing something worthwhile with her knowledge.

Early in 1957 the upwardly mobile Yip family finally achieved a change of residence which would take them to the summit of Hong Kong Island and install them in elegant accommodation still owned by Teddy today. Their first-floor flat in Repulse Bay Mansions, a Thirties' apartment block, is airy and spacious. The deep balcony, brimming with hibiscus, geraniums and lush green foliage, looks out across the magnificent Repulse Bay, situated on the far side of the island. The interior looks much as it did when the Yips first made it their home. Teddy's superstitious beliefs have meant that nothing can ever be thrown away for fear of throwing out his luck with it so even though the chairs and sofas have been replaced and re-upholstered more than once, small pieces of the original wood and fabric are incorporated into the new pieces. Fine furniture stands on floors of polished wood; the drawing room leads through into the dining room through a wide archway. One side of the drawing room is covered by a vast glass-fronted cabinet holding all Teddy's motor-racing trophies. Placed at right angles to this and centrally hung in a white expanse of wall is a blown-up head and shoulders photographic portrait of Teddy in his racing gear. Below it there is a splendidly ornate gold and silver cup.

Susie and her children did not spend many months in this flat. She had recently taken Tina and George on a trip to England to scout out the possibilities of taking up residence there. After some searching, Susie decided that she would ask Teddy to buy them a house in East Grinstead in Sussex. It had been recommended to her by some English friends she had made on the voyage who were retiring there after a lifetime spent in Shanghai.

In the summer of 1957 they packed their bags, crated up some furniture and set sail on the SS Hamburg for England. Betty was left behind to keep her father company, but became so homesick that she soon followed the others.

4

Rescue

❖

W E'LL TAKE HER to Timbuctoo if necessary,' wrote Tim in a postscript to Vicky's letter to Alison in August 1982, sent while they were waiting for the results of the biopsy. Vicky was being marvellously positive, so he would try and be positive too. Like Vicky he felt better when he was doing something but they both knew deep down that hope hung by a very slender thread. The future was a void too awful to contemplate. The surgeons had said the tumour was inoperable and it was doubtful that anything else could be done, except possibly some radiotherapy as a palliative measure.

Wednesday, 25th August dawned and suddenly, extraordinarily, everything changed. The biopsy result came through: it was, as expected, an advanced ovarian cancer. About as bad as it could be. And yet, was it? The tumour was well differentiated which meant that though large it was contained and might, therefore, respond to chemotherapy. That very same afternoon, at five o'clock, into the ward and up to her bed, walked someone who was, from that day forward, to play a leading role in Vicky's life. He had something quite special to offer her, a slight but real chance of cure if she was prepared to go through a particularly powerful course of chemotherapy.

Dr Maurice Slevin was then a newly appointed consultant

28

physician specializing in medical oncology (the treatment of cancer with drugs) at St Bartholomew's Hospital and at the Homerton Hospital in Hackney. The treatment he proposed was dire: a potent cocktail of three cytotoxic (anti-cancer) drugs – cisplatin, doxorubicin and cyclophosphamide – to be administered in three courses over three months with the aim of shrinking the tumour enough to remove it surgically. The operation, an oopherectomy, would mean removing her ovaries and womb, and thus all hope of having the children she and Tim had so much wanted. It would then be followed up with a further three months' course to remove the remaining cancer. He warned her that with all this to go through, the best chance of success he could offer her was no more than one in five; in other words, the possibility of remission (perhaps permanent) was a mere twenty per cent.

Vicky was not Teddy Yip's daughter for nothing. Among other things she had inherited from her father was his keen gambling instinct and his determination to win: whatever the cost, at all costs. For the last week she had been living under a sentence of death. The promise that Dr Slevin was now holding out to her was nothing less than miraculous. As she later described it to Anthony Clare, it was as if 'somebody, suddenly appears on the horizon with a boat and some food and water'. The drowning castaway had been offered a lifeline and she grabbed hold of it eagerly.

She knew, of course, that an arduous and dangerous journey lay ahead. In that first long meeting with Maurice Slevin she asked him to explain in considerable detail the procedures, the research behind the treatment, the odds, the risks and all the possible side effects she should expect. She questioned him on every point, taking copious notes throughout their talk. He had never before met a patient like her.

They took to each other immediately. Both young – he was a year her junior – both brilliant, both very ambitious and deeply involved in their careers, they had much in common and swiftly found they were talking to each other more as if they were meeting socially than as doctor and patient. Maurice's normal custom was to allow a first meeting with a new patient to last for a maximum of one hour. On this occasion, he was so knocked sideways by Vicky's overwhelming enthusiasm – 'she was really quite over the top', he recalls – that he stayed on and on. Two and a half hours later he 'crawled out, having heard her whole life story, told in her usual immodest way'.

From that day forward they were to be firm friends, and ultimately allies and partners in the joint enterprise of founding BACUP, although neither could possibly have foreseen that particular outcome on that long ago summer afternoon. There were to be some tricky moments in their relationship but Vicky never wavered in her loyalty to Maurice as her doctor. She was to be a difficult, demanding patient, telephoning him once, often twice a day to tell him about something new she had read or heard about, or to reel off a list of questions. At the beginning of her illness, even as a doctor she knew very little about cancer, so her questions tended to be relatively naïve, but she was soon reading up everything relevant that she could lay her hands on. Every week an envelope would drop on his desk containing copies of all the papers relating to ovarian cancer – underlined and annotated – that she had found in the various medical journals. This continued for about two months by which time he estimates that she was probably better read in the subject than any ovarian oncologist. However, once she knew all there was to be known she moved on to something else. The telephone calls, however, did not cease.

Someone less self-assured than Maurice Slevin might have taken this appetite for information as a sign that she lacked confidence in him but he guessed, correctly, that it was not mistrust in him that lay behind her persistent ferreting. Vicky had an absolute need to feel in control and the only way she could achieve that satisfactorily as far as her illness was concerned was by knowing as much as possible about it. He urged her several times to seek a second opinion because he naturally felt responsible for the difficult treatment he was proposing and he was concerned that she should at least consider other less drastic options. Through her family connections she was in touch with doctors all over the world who were telephoning her with their opinions but Vicky was never in any doubt that Maurice Slevin was the doctor for her. She might have been rigorously questioning but in the end she always deferred to the opinion of 'my medical oncologist' as she was wont to call him in typically proprietorial fashion. Maurice put up with Vicky's sometimes quite impossibly high-handed behaviour – demands which he admits he would not have tolerated from any other patient – for two simple reasons: he liked her and he found her fascinating. It was an attraction that was never to wane.

That first meeting was followed by several more with Tim taking notes as well as Vicky. They were elated and thrilled beyond measure. Suddenly the world had changed its dismal hue and Vicky could hope to look beyond her birthday. She had a manic streak in her personality which had been becoming more evident over the years. Now she was made positively euphoric by news which others might have found more sobering, even alarming. It was, after all, a comparatively slim chance of success that she was being offered and to achieve it she would have to endure considerable pain, discomfort and the loss of her fertility. She knew all this with her head but she had yet to absorb it fully with her heart and her soul.

That first night after meeting Maurice Vicky found it impossible to sleep. At two o'clock in the morning she was writing a list of all the things she would do now that she had been given this reprieve. It was to be nothing less than putting the world to rights: her world of friends, family and colleagues. There were political wranglings and misunderstandings to be sorted out in the workplace; marriages to be repaired; family relationships to be restored; friendships to be revived. The builders had finished working in their Berkshire cottage. She would make the curtains, buy the furniture, paint the walls and plant the garden: in short, do everything she had been meaning to do for months before this last bout of illness but had failed to find the energy. Now she knew she had the chance of living, all her former zest for life came flooding back; it was so palpable, it was as if she had been given a blood transfusion.

When Tim came the following morning to fetch her home she showed him her list: thirty-six objectives, most of them quite specific but included was her determination to do something about cancer. What precisely that was to be was not yet clear to her but she resented the way her cancer had 'shut her into a closet'.

Already in this first week she had experienced its distancing effect through the reactions of doctors and others around her, and these, after all, were professionals used to dealing with cancer patients. Later, many times both privately and in public, for instance, in her interviews with Anthony Clare and Terry Wogan, she was to describe how hurtfully a few friends had behaved on hearing the news of her cancer. They had simply drifted away and never renewed contact with her again. She had naturally felt very upset at the time but later, as she began to understand more about her disease and its effects and talked to other cancer patients, she realized that, sadly, this was an all too common reaction. It was not so much her they were shutting off but the face of death that she was forcing them to look at. Vicky herself, in that early time immediately after the results of the biopsy, actually felt better in a strange kind of way. She knew now what was wrong with her and she had been offered some weapons to deal with the enemy. Why, then, did most people insist on treating her as if she were a condemned prisoner? She was not going to stand for it.

She got going on her list even before she left hospital, calling in one or two people to discuss her 'plan'. Others, she telephoned from her bedside, warning them that she intended to sort them out, in the nicest possible way of course. When Vicky meant business, she got down to it immediately. She saw no point in wasting time on polite beating about the bush. She saw a problem; she would find the solution. A friend who had good cause to appreciate Vicky's problem-solving capacities, said later of her: 'Vicky absolutely loved a problem. It was like throwing a bone to a dog. She would worry at it until she had worked out the way to beat it.'

Such was the force of Vicky's personality combined with her genuine good will, that on the whole people accepted her interventions with a good grace. To refuse would have seemed churlish; it is always disarming to have someone take so much thought for your wellbeing. She admits, though, in a letter to Alison and Michael written the following Sunday, when she had ticked several more 'problems' off her list that Tim was expressing some misgivings. 'He doesn't like this ruthless streak to use my illness but I feel that if it is for everyone's good I should do it . . . hope you agree.'

It would not have made much difference whatever their response might have been. Vicky was convinced that she was doing what she ought to do; nothing, therefore, would have deflected her from her chosen course of action. Her cancer had pulled her up in her own tracks. It had forced her to look at her own life in a completely new light, and to reconsider her ambitions and her priorities.

She wanted to share her insights and her new perspective with those who were close to her. She had already had several intimate discussions with Tim and David about life and death;

she had confided some of her feelings to one or two of her closer hospital colleagues. To Alison she had put in some long transatlantic telephone calls, much of the time being taken up with her feelings about her religion. Although she was still a practising Catholic Vicky hated the sense of guilt she had come to associate with it. Each time she had fallen ill she wondered what she had done to deserve the 'punishment'. Cancer seemed the final and most devastating blow from an angry God, but why? She examined her life carefully and could honestly find little cause for His wrath. It was true, she did not always go to church on Sundays. It was also true that she had a very close friendship with a man other than her husband but this was no guilty secret.

For eight years she had been sharing part of her life with David; many of the leisure hours that Tim, the fully committed politician and business man, could not spare. With David she could play the piano and talk about gardens and food and ideas outside the narrow medical track. He fed a side of Vicky's nature that she knew she was in danger of starving in her single-minded pursuit of her career. David was a soul mate, as Alison was in her way, as Tim was in his way: each in their different ways were indispensable to Vicky. The great advantage that David could offer her was his undivided attention. It was true he was a busy GP and he had many other friends, but he was not married and he was prepared to put Vicky before other claims on his time. He lived nearby and, if need be, he could drop everything and be at her side.

'I believe he is part of some divine plan for me – to look after me and help Timmy through my illness,' she wrote to Alison on that last Sunday in August with a prescience she could not then have imagined.

It was wonderful to be home again. Vicky and Tim had lived in Northbourne Road on the south side of Clapham Common since 1978. Their house was in an elegant, early Victorian terrace, set well back from the leafy residential road in a pretty garden with steps leading up to the front door. On that same Thursday, 26th August, that she arrived home, Vicky notes in her diary that David had helped her mother Susie find a flat in the vicinity. This is where Susie would live for the next few years, apart from occasional trips back to Australia, whither she had emigrated, and to Hong Kong. She was to find the damp English weather a great trial for her arthritis but she was determined that she would do all she could for her daughter. And she did. 'I have never seen a more devoted mother,' comments a close family friend.

The next few days were 'hectic' to quote a much used word at that time in Vicky's cryptic diaries. On the Friday, she managed to walk downstairs and she 'sent' two musical friends out on a mission to find her an electric piano. Her sister Tina arrived from Switzerland and there followed long chats with her and a couple of friends. On the Saturday, while Tim went down to the cottage to make a list of what needed to be done to make it habitable, she stayed in bed because her pain had come back. The visitors kept coming, much to her delight. Many of them were on her list so she was able to get going on her self-appointed task of putting their lives in order. She was continuing the peacemaking role she had first learnt as a child within her own family. Whenever a childish quarrel blew up Vicky was the one the others would turn to and expect to mediate between the warring parties. Vicky, they knew, would remain calm, dispassionate, above all fair. Once she had weighed up the rights and wrongs of the dispute and sorted out the differences, she could be relied upon, by a process of persuasion and reasoning, to resolve the problem and dispense a just decision which they could all accept.

Vicky firmly believed that problems could always be solved if only people would tackle them with the tools of reason rather than the weapons of passion. Although she was always ready to fight on behalf of others, she was not so good at standing up for herself, again a trait that was to stay with her for life. She would always prefer to walk away from a potentially antagonistic situation if it was clear that the only person under threat was herself. This was not because she was a moral coward – show the cause to be a just one and Vicky would be the first to nail her colours to the mast – but as far as she personally was concerned there was always this deep-seated dread of being found out in some way; it would not be in wrongdoing because she took care to avoid that. No, her real fear was that she would be confirmed as the worthless person her father's attitude towards her had always suggested she was. An open conflict might expose her and bring down unbearable scorn and odium upon her.

Vicky's reluctance to handle any conflict directly involving her was to cause problems for her but that comes later on in the story of her life. What it reveals about her is that the apparently cool and rational Vicky had her emotional Achilles' heel like anyone else.

On Sunday morning she rose at five o'clock when Tim and her mother were still sleeping and pottered downstairs to enjoy the garden and defrost the freezer, admitting in her letter to Alison that she rather enjoyed chipping off the ice and sweeping up the bits while no one could rag her. The electronic piano arrived and was played, with great delight. It would be a constant companion, at home and in hospital, in the years to come. She lay on the sofa all day, receiving more friends and their children. Life stories were recounted. Friends unburdened themselves to her; she felt lapped in their love. The house was warm and humming with life. Susie prepared delicious Chinese meals; Tim carried trays up and downstairs; children tumbled underfoot; everyone tried to help. Hectic ... hectic ... and so it went on until Tuesday evening, the last day of the month.

Tomorrow she would be going into Barts for her first course of chemotherapy. She could not say she was looking forward to the treatment but she longed to start living again.

'I think I may get Tim to get a special tree to plant to commemorate my illness and recovery!' she wrote to Alison. She felt happier about her religious feelings, even if they were not completely resolved. She decided she did not know any more about God, at least not the God the nuns and her parents had taught her to worship. On the telephone she had expressed strong feelings to Alison and now the guilt had gone; it had been banished together with her Catholic beliefs. She was left with 'just a feeling of something spiritual that exists and watches over us'. She felt at peace with herself.

5

Bald Eagle

❖

A NEW LIFE STARTED for Vicky on 1st September 1982. Although she felt that her two previous illnesses had served as a rehearsal for the big C, nothing could really have prepared her for what was now to come.

The anti-cancer drugs prescribed for her by Dr Slevin were indeed powerful. Cisplatin is a derivative of platinum and she had been forewarned that it would cause nausea and vomiting and that in due course her hair would probably fall out. What she did not expect was the intensity of the reaction she would sustain that very first night after her first injection. She had been fitted with a cold cap which is a form of ice-pack folded in towels and is worn by the patient before, during and after the treatment as a way of trying to reduce hair loss. It works by temporarily narrowing the blood vessels in the scalp and so reduces the amount of drug reaching the hair follicles. She had also been given an antidote to the vomiting.

'Typical doctor,' she recalled. 'I got all the worst side-effects.' The cap slipped down and caused an appalling headache. The antidote gave her what is termed in medical terminology an occulo-gyro crisis. Her eyes rotated upwards and she became quite immobile, unable to move a limb or speak a word. She could find no way to explain to the nurses what was happening but it felt as if the end of the world was about to happen there in the ward. Eventually, she managed to convey to the houseman that she needed Tim who was called out in the early hours of the morning to sort out the matter. In fact, Maurice Slevin had anticipated this possible reaction and had left precise instructions for dealing with it but in the crisis they were overlooked. Vicky was to go through many worse ordeals but the memory of this one still made her shudder at the end of her life.

Three days later when the worst effects had worn off, Tim took her home where Susie was keeping house. The round of visitors started up again but this time Vicky was feeling rather low and debilitated. All the same, she was able to record eating a boiled egg without vomiting on the Saturday, and on Sunday afternoon she enjoyed a tea of sandwiches and lemon meringue pie followed later by a chicken dinner with David. It was typical of Vicky to record her menus; she loved her food with unashamed gusto and it had long been a habit to note what she had eaten in the company of friends and family.

Vicky herself admitted that in this respect she was Chinese through and through. 'From the moment they wake up,' she once said towards the end of her life, 'the Chinese are either eating food, preparing food, thinking about food, looking at food, reading about food or talking about food.'

Another frequent diary item in these months of chemo- therapy and its aftermath refers to children: 'crept to kids' bed 7.30 – played' or something similar appears quite often and means literally that. Vicky loved playing games with children – the child in her was never far below the surface – and children, of course, recognizing her genuine empathy with them, responded to her enthusiasm and interest. Vicky would happily spend hours with them playing Monopoly, chess, racing demon or whatever else was the fancy of the moment. She and Tim had decided that since they could have no children of their own they would fill the house with nephews and nieces, god children, and any other children around, all of whom were always made welcome. They would enjoy their friends' children and be grateful that they did not have the everyday chores of bringing up a family.

Alison and Michael's first child, a son, was born that September. He too was to be one of Vicky's god children and there were letters and telephone calls and photographs describing his arrival and first weeks of life. There is no doubt that Vicky was thrilled for her best friend but mixed with that joy was also some sorrow. She and Alison had always said they would have their children as near in age as possible so they could grow up together and become great friends like their mothers. But it was not to be and both women felt keenly the bitter irony that while Alison had been gestating her son, Vicky had been growing her cancer. Vicky was sad but apparently neither angry nor jealous, both emotions which would have been understandable in the circumstances.

Some people close to her did wonder whether Vicky, so dedicated to her career, would ever really have wanted to take the time off to start a family. When Anthony Clare asked her that question she replied that the loss of children had to be thought about in several ways. Cancer had forced her to face her own mortality; it was, therefore, very hard indeed that it should also be denying her the opportunity to give her husband something to remember her by, in case she should die. Both she and Tim, she explained with a chuckle in her voice, were somewhat dynastic, coming from old families who believed in handing things down to the next generation. On the other hand, and here the ever-practical Vicky comes to the fore, she did wonder: 'How I would have coped if I had had young children during this illness,' and added, 'how much more time we've had for each other, my husband and I, because we've not had to worry about those problems.'

We have to remember also that she was talking to Anthony Clare more than two years after the event and so had had time to rationalize her feelings. Moreover, so much else had happened to Vicky in the interim that that particular loss, although it would never be forgotten, had undoubtedly receded and diminished. But in September 1983 with two more courses of chemotherapy to go through before she could be considered ready for the operation Vicky had a more immediate loss to face.

Her hair was beginning to fall out. Thick, black and lustrous, she had always been proud of it. Her first mention of what was happening is a diary note on 20th September but it had been coming out in handfuls for days. 'For two weeks I was in tears every morning, plucking the clumps of hair from all over the bedclothes; and while I was trying to lead a normal life I had the embarrassing experience of hair falling into my mine-strone. Intellectually I understood what was happening, but emotionally it reinforced my feelings that I was losing a part of myself.'

This experience, so shattering for any cancer patient, was described in her article for the *British Medical Journal* and made a deep and lasting impression on Vicky. Right to the end of her life she would recall the distressing memory of lunching with her mother in an Italian restaurant and feeling her hair slide off her head like great wodges of melting ice into the soup. What particularly shattered her was that although she had been told it would happen no one had warned her how dreadful she would feel about it.

'There were thousands of patients who had been there,' she said to me. 'They had experienced it but they hadn't conveyed it to other people. Why weren't they telling their doctors what was it like? Look at me. I had this marvellous caring team of people looking after me in Barts and of course they told me I would lose my hair, but they had no idea about the real problems.'

Vicky, the doctor, had found it hard to understand that

patients often have great difficulty in communicating such personal problems to their doctors. They are anxious not to worry them about 'trifles' which it might seem ungracious to mention since they are so fully involved with giving life-saving care and treatment. Vicky, the patient, now understood that there was this yawning gap in communication and began to understand why. Her own trauma made her realize how much people needed to talk and to share their problems. The doctors were not succeeding in bridging the gap. There must be some other means of giving people the information they wanted. But what could it be? Meanwhile, Vicky the fighter was determined not to be defeated by her distressing experience.

A fellow patient suggested she wear a hair net at night so that the falling hair could at least be contained. She never felt comfortable with her wig so out of doors she wore a tweed fisherman's hat she had bought at W. Bill and indoors she did not bother with anything. As her treatment progressed and her hair became thin and tufty she wondered whether she could not somehow make a virtue out of necessity. She discussed it with David. Why not shave it all off, he suggested, and be done with it? No sooner said than done.

So one afternoon he escorted her to his own barber, the discreet and gentlemanly Truefitt and Hill in Old Bond Street. As they entered he had a moment of panic. 'My friend is a lady,' he confided to the receptionist. 'No problem,' came the unperturbed answer.

Vicky was led to the back where a spacious private cubicle, lined with oak panelling and mirrors hidden from the other clients by burgundy velvet curtains, gave her privacy. David waited with some trepidation for her to emerge but Vicky was delighted with the result. Now completely shorn, she was accompanied by David to the British Home Stores where she bought a grey trilby hat – a style that was to become very much her own – for a modest £2.50.

They celebrated the occasion with a slap-up lunch at the Neal Street restaurant in Covent Garden. The atmosphere was hot and halfway through the meal Vicky had had enough. She whisked off her hat, revealing her shaven head to the assembled diners who, in true British fashion, looked and gasped and looked away again, not sure whether they were seeing an exotic model or a boy Buddhist monk. Delighted with her effect, from then on Vicky called herself 'the bald eagle'.

On one later occasion she did try for something more feminine in that shrine to upper class wealth, Fortnum and Mason's, but something about the mirrors and pastels and cutglass vowels tinkling on the scented air brought out the devil in her. Approaching the supercilious saleswoman in the hat department, she said with her usual directness. 'I'd like a hat. As you can see, I desperately need one,' whereupon she whipped off the one she was wearing to expose her bald pate. Collapse of saleswoman.

Vicky had a pronounced sense of style. Those who knew her later were familiar with the small androgynous figure who nearly always wore a smart man's shirt under tailored tweed jacket with a skirt or well cut trousers. As her illness advanced and she had to accommodate various tubes and bags around her body, she found it was a style which made it easier for her both to conceal and handle them. It also suited her.

But it had not always been so. In her days as a medical student at Cambridge Vicky was renowned for her dazzling and expensive wardrobe. Tim, who met her there for the first time in 1968 during her first week, recalls in particular a pair of thigh-length red leather boots. There were also suede coats, silk shirts, model dresses and masses of shoes and handbags, bought for her by her mother.

'Almost as many as Arianna Stassanopolis who had the room next door,' commented Alison, who was Vicky's exact contemporary.

Alison and Vicky had met several months before when they had come up for interview at Girton on the same day. Vicky was a knock-out in a very short skirt, jumper and shirt worn in a combination of shocking pink and turquoise. Her straight black hair hung round her face and down her back. She was extremely pretty and, despite the daring outfit, looked as innocent as indeed she was. Alison, who came from a provincial Northern background, felt like a humble sparrow next to this exotic bird of paradise but they fell into conversation and hit it off extraordinarily well from the start.

Vicky changed her style quite deliberately when she moved to London and began studying for her MD at St Thomas' Hospital. She wore simple skirts with shirts or jumpers under her white coat, low-heeled shoes and very little make-up. She aimed to look as ordinary and as like any other junior house officer as possible. Her mother despaired of her: 'I used to tell her she was a disgrace,' she said, with a laugh, to me. 'She would wear the same clothes for years. I remember a pair of Dr Scholl sandals that she always took with her on holiday. And, can you believe it, when she got married she was still wearing the bra she had when she was twelve.'

Like so many stories about Vicky, these about her clothes reveal some of the contradictions that were so much part of her personality. Even at her most casual, she was highly fastidious about her appearance, in part because she had a natural feminine vanity which made her want to look her best. Creating an image also mattered to her. She knew how important it was to convey the right impression in the right places.

Vicky was also a very frugal person, at least as far as spending money on herself was concerned. Whereas she was remarkable for her unobtrusive generosity to her friends she never saw the point of throwing anything out – clothes or possessions of any kind – if they still had some use in them. Maybe this parsimony had been branded into her from her early childhood years of poverty before her father made his fortune. Her sister Tina confesses to the same hoarding instincts.

Vicky was never one of those people who let themselves go when they feel under the weather, though, heaven knows, she spent so much time in hospital beds that she would have had good reason to lose interest, even if only temporarily, in her appearance. And sometimes she would be as manic as her father in her capacity to spend, spend, spend.

During the autumn of 1982 Vicky had another project in hand to keep her mind off the pain, the sickness and the chronic fatigue induced by the chemotherapy. Their cottage near Hungerford was awaiting her final touches which would make it possible for them to move in the furniture and start spending weekends there.

She drove down to it one Sunday in late September with her mother when Tim was at the annual Liberal conference. It was her first visit since the builders had been in and it enabled her to decide on the wallpaper and take measurements for the curtains. Her second dose of chemotherapy at the end of September made her feel very low for several days so for a while it was Tim who made the flying weekend trips to inspect such things as the installation of the radiators and the hanging of the wallpaper. Finally, as October drew on and she recovered her strength, she felt she was ready to tackle a proper weekend at the cottage.

Friday, 22nd October found her packing. After cooking lunch for David, she and Tim drove down to the cottage that evening. Her diary entries say it all:

First night! I cook wurst and mushroom soup in rice cooker.

23rd October – Saturday
Wake 6 am at cottage very excited – shop Newbury am, TV, toaster, etc. Nursery – lunch first time 5 Bells – nap – plant bulbs and new plants. Malcolm and Jamie and Sarah – I invite them to drinks. I make fire and cook bacon, egg, baked beans and tidy kitchen.

24th October – Sunday
This weekend feel human first time in two months. Wake 7 am excited – tidy house and organize kitchen. Home 10 pm – super day.

The excitement boiled over to Monday when she spent a busy day with her sister Betty visiting Habitat, Laura Ashley, and similar shops to buy furniture and furnishing materials. And it carried her through her third and final dose of chemotherapy on the Wednesday. She was home again by Thursday evening and even though there were the usual draining episodes of vomiting and nausea, all recorded, on Friday morning she was ordering logs, top soil and turf for the cottage garden. On Saturday she was cutting out the bedroom curtains with her mother and her friend Pauline who had come from Paris to see her, while Betty did all the ironing. On Sunday and throughout the following week she and her mother were frenziedly sewing curtains. By Friday, 5th November, only ten days after her chemotherapy, and having slept very little the night before because she was so excited, once more she was packing for a weekend in the cottage.

This time she went down with David and on the Saturday her mother, Tim and other friends turned up for their first lunch at the new table she had bought from the Pine shop. Afterwards Vicky dug the garden and when everyone had left she put up some curtains before cooking supper for herself and Tim. She went to bed at eleven noting that she was tired!

The Sunday was similarly occupied with she and Tim doing jobs around the house; a friend came to lunch and Vicky worked in the garden until it got too dark and they drove home in a traffic jam. 'Bed 9.30 – knackered!' she notes.

Not surprisingly, she was exhausted after the weekend and had to spend two days catching up on sleep but it was worth it and soon she was back at the sewing machine, making more curtains, interspersed with more shopping and visits to Barts for tests to see whether the tumour had reduced. It had and her operation was booked for Thursday, 25th November – three months to the day from her last one – but she was determined that the cottage would be pristine by that date.

The last weekend before she went into hospital was quite frantic. After packing her suitcase ready for hospital, she planted bulbs in the front garden at Northbourne Road, then drove down to the cottage with Tim and had a pub lunch before going to the nursery for some more plants and returning to the cottage in time to welcome her sister Betty with her two young sons for tea. On Sunday they had guests as well and when they arrived back in Clapham she spent the evening with David playing duets.

It was a tearful and sad ending to another crowded, happy weekend. Tomorrow she had to go into hospital for still more tests before her operation on Thursday and who could tell what the results of that would be.

Although the driving force behind all this activity was Vicky, she could not have achieved all she did in those first months, and even more so later, had she not been so wholeheartedly and unselfishly helped by her family. They were doing it the way Vicky and Tim wanted it to be. It might be thought that all Vicky's intense activity was merely an escape route out of accepting the gravity of her illness but she and Tim knew full well what they were doing. They both recognized that Vicky coped best when she had a project that fully occupied her.

'The Chinese extended family aint half bad,' commented Tim on one occasion. He should know, having had much cause to appreciate the loving support they offered him as well. Vicky, however, was not so good at saying thank you, especially to those closest to her, like her mother and sisters. Indeed, she could be thoroughly wearing for everyone. A perfectionist herself, she was demanding and bossy, constantly asking for things to be brought to her in the bedroom or pointing out missing items on the tray that had just been brought up several floors from the basement kitchen. Her mother spent long hours cooking and when Vicky was in hospital she would put a hot meal in the car and drive through the London traffic to Barts or Homerton Hospital in Hackney, whichever place Vicky happened to be. Either she or Betty, who lived some thirty miles away in East Grinstead, would prepare home-made chicken soup every day.

Susie was always at Vicky's disposal and her one concern was her daughter's happiness. She has a gentle and giving nature and the last thing she wanted to do was to walk into her daughter's house and reorganize the routines but inevitably, two women in one kitchen tend to tread on each other's toes. Vicky would come down and find her cupboard rearranged or something out of order and get very irritated.

Tina, who was then divorced and living in Zurich with her two children where she was working in a bank, went part-time so that she could spend half the week in Clapham with her sister and add her help to the family pool. Although Vicky loved being the centre of attention and the person to whom everyone confided their problems, there were times when she found she could not take any more. It was especially difficult when she was feeling debilitated from her chemotherapy and the family were rowing between each other. 'Tired and miserable,' she notes on a bad day in October. 'All too much family.'

Tim was not a natural nurse, although in time he was to become very adept at carrying out the sick room rituals. However, at the beginning of Vicky's cancer treatment he was very pressured in his job with London Weekend Television and the stress was compounded by his political engagements as a prospective parliamentary candidate. He was frequently out in the evenings and would return home late, very tired and hungry. Vicky might have been on her own, waiting for him, feeling ill and steadily becoming more depressed.

Sometimes, she might have passed a few hours with David, or her mother or some other friend but she was finding it very hard to tolerate this kind of disorganized life in her present invalid state.

It had been all right when they were both in full spate with their careers. 'It was a *folie à deux*,' said Alison. 'They were both moving very fast in quite different directions and the faster one went one way, the faster the other would go the other way. Just occasionally they came together.' That kind of freneticism suited them both, indeed it positively inspired and stimulated them. This was fine when they were both in peak mental and physical condition but one player was no longer fit.

Vicky had been seriously ill for almost two years now and the strain was beginning to tell on both of them. Tears and rows and what Vicky called 'grumps' were recorded in the diary but so also were the reconciliations. However, they both knew that they would have to reconsider their way of life. It could not go on like this.

David was a tower of strength throughout this time as he would always be to the end of her life. He too was ever at her disposal: ready to go out shopping with her; help her plant bulbs in the garden; wash her hair for her; cook her a tasty meal; take her to a restaurant; play duets with her when she felt up to it. He was a wonderful companion to share all the quiet domestic pleasures of life that Vicky was beginning to enjoy so much.

Living with a sick person is never easy and new habits have to be learned and adjustments made. Although Vicky had 'trained' her husband and David in something of what to expect through the earlier gruelling illnesses, the cancer with its life-threatening implications was different. It hung like a lowering storm cloud over all their lives.

Vicky, with her will to survive and win through against all the odds was determined to behave as if it was not really happening, but even she, with all her genuine optimism, could not avoid the dark moments when depression and fear overwhelmed her. There were many tears and many tensions in those months which only those close to her saw and could help her through. Long chats about cancer and death are frequently recorded in the diary. The contents of those heart-to-heart talks remain with her confidants but it is clear that Vicky, a very private person, was thinking deeply about fundamental matters. The Vicky the outside world saw remained positive and ebullient.

6

Crossing the Divide

❖

VICKY WALKED INTO the Pitcairn ward at Barts Hospital on Monday morning, 22nd November, looking trim and composed. She put her briefcase on the floor beside her locker and pulled off her hat, laying it on the bed.

Sue, lying in the bed opposite, was stunned. Goodness, she thought, that's what I must look like when 'it's' not on. She felt her wig tentatively, hoping it was still in place. She never bared her head for an instant, only swapping the wig for a scarf at night when the lights were off. She had not looked at herself in a mirror since the awful time a few weeks back after her second course of chemotherapy when her father had helped her to wash her hair. He was combing it through when suddenly it slid in great blonde swatches off her head.

Vicky by now had undressed and climbed into bed. She took some papers out of her case and became very absorbed in them. She was doing her bank accounts and totting up the costs of renovating the cottage. To Sue, she radiated an aura of 'don't come near me'.

Sue picked up her book. Vicky picked up hers. After a while, Sue peered round hers. What a coincidence! The Chinese girl was reading Dick Francis, just like her. Without further ado, she got out of bed, marched over to Vicky and said: 'I'm glad to see someone of my age having chemotherapy.'

Vicky looked over the top of her book and asked: 'How old are you?'

'Twenty-four and my name's Sue.'

'I'm thirty-two and I'm a doctor,' came the response. (For some unexplained reason Vicky always dropped a year off her age when talking about her cancer. She was in fact approaching her thirty-fourth birthday at the time.)

So what, about being a doctor, Sue was tempted to respond, but she resisted.

They started talking to each other and compared notes. The Dick Francis connection was a great icebreaker because it turned out that Sue, a policewoman, was a keen rider and kept her own horse in Essex. Vicky had just discovered the author and was especially enjoying the racy novel she was currently reading because it was set in and around the Lambourn valley near her cottage.

Both young women had ovarian cancer; they had both had three courses of chemotherapy already; and they were both booked to have their operation on the same day followed by a further regimen of chemotherapy. There the similarities ended. They came from very different backgrounds but they found each other intriguing and, as often happens on a ward, sickness breaks down all barriers. Their youth was a bond and Vicky was disarmed by Sue's irreverent sense of fun. They soon became the blue-eyed girls of the ward.

'I used to mickey-take her mercilessly,' Sue said. 'She would order me around, click her fingers and point to whatever she wanted. One day, seeing her sitting up in bed with her little round head, eyes darting indignant looks and little mouth turned down, I said, "Oh my gawd! You look just like ET!"'

Vicky must have been one of the few people in the world who did not know who ET was, at least she pretended she did not know, but she enjoyed the joke and riposted by calling Sue 'Grasshopper' after a Buddhist monk in a David Carradine film. The name stuck and in a letter to Alison Vicky was urging her to see the ET film. 'Everyone says I'm like it — lovable but pathetic!'

'I always knew that this was a brain working on a much higher level,' said Sue, 'but at the same time she could be quite naïve. She used to tell me how brilliant she was and that her father was a millionaire, not boastfully, but just to let me know the kind of person she was. She was horrified at first to be on an open NHS ward — she'd always been in a side room before. And do you know, she had never eaten marmite or tomato ketchup before I introduced them to her?' Vicky probably had but she enjoyed playing up to Sue's preconceptions.

The big East End policewoman and the petite Chinese doctor became firm friends. Vicky went down first on Thursday morning for the operation. Both were to go through the same ordeal. The surgeon hoped to remove all visible sign of their tumours but to achieve that their ovaries and their wombs would also have to go. Both of them understood the implications — no chance of children and an early, artificial menopause — but they had also been warned that they might have to have a colostomy as well. This would mean living with a bag for the rest of their lives. Sue found herself praying the night before: 'Please God, don't let me have a colostomy' and then remembers admonishing herself, 'this is ridiculous if it means you live . . .' So she added: 'But if I must, please let me be able to cope with it.'

When she came round, she found herself full of tubes and in great pain, but, thank God, no bag! Terry, her best friend, was prancing up and down the ward with delight and relief for her. Sue had always twitted Vicky on being the wimp, the one to whom everything seemed to happen but now, she looked across from her bed of agony to see Vicky sitting up in bed calmly eating a bacon sandwich.

That was probably the first and only time that Vicky had the physical advantage of Sue. The next few days were very up and down for both of them. There was a lot of pain, they were having to cope with hot flushes as well and in two weeks' time they would have to have another course of chemotherapy. Even so, they managed to amuse themselves in between the bad times.

Vicky had a musical calculator on which she could punch out simple tunes and Sue could sing, so they decided they would go round the wards offering patients a Christmas carol of their choice picked from a scroll hand-painted by Sue. Both bald, painfully thin and wearing striped rugby shirts ending just above their knees which had been given to them by Sue's friends back at the police station, they looked rather like escapees from a concentration camp.

'Flat chested and knobbly kneed,' said Sue. 'We looked dreadful but we had fun and we raised £67 for the ward. Vicky was a mini dynamo.'

The chemotherapy seemed like the last straw for both of them and they were very sick. Sue remembers Vicky hobbling out of the ward clutching her sick bowl. It was Sunday, 12th December and, like ET, she wanted to go home.

It was marvellous to be back in her own bedroom even if she was still vomiting. Her brother George was there with his wife and baby son Andrew; friends came round; she played the piano; and, just as a spot of occupational therapy, she darned fourteen of Tim's socks.

The two friends arranged to see each other again after Christmas when their next course of chemotherapy was due. They met twice more in hospital and then Sue was pronounced clear of cancer.

Today she is a healthy happy woman, married to a policeman and with two stepsons to look after. She has given up her career in the force and does not ride any more but she has become a successful water colourist and portrait painter, a talent she discovered when she was in hospital.

Vicky never forgot Sue. When she spoke about her to me five years later her face lit up and she betrayed not a trace of bitterness that Sue should be cured while she had been so much less lucky. She also understood why Sue no longer wanted to be involved with anything that reminded her of cancer. She had done her bit by helping to set up a support group near her home in Essex but, once it was going well, she left it, believing that her best way of coping was to get through the illness and then put it behind her. She also made a magnificent fund-raising effort for Barts Hospital by bicycling from Land's End to John O'Groats to raise money for a CT scanner, an achievement that Vicky, not Sue, told me about.

Sue's bounce and her extrovert cheerfulness appealed enormously to Vicky who was like her in some respects, and yet so unalike. Where Sue was forthcoming Vicky would be inclined to hold back. In those early days of her illness, though less so later, there was a quality of reserve and 'hands off' about Vicky that some people found intimidating. Not Sue. Earthy, warm, she took a hearty delight in teasing Vicky but she knew just how far she could go. She might call her a wimp but she was in fact inspired by Vicky's courage.

Before the operation Sue had implored the nurses not to let the scarf slip off her head. Afterwards, lying in bed and groaning with pain, and later, vomiting ceaselessly, she thought, why bother? Her friend Terry painted her bald pate in punkish colours and her moment of total liberation came when she, a humble WPC, was visited by her Chief Constable, bald as an egg himself.

'Aha!' he said. 'I see you're in disguise.'

'Snap!' she replied.

After that, she always wore a cloth cap or hat of some kind and brazened out the stares she received on the Underground and when she returned to her beat.

What Vicky learnt from Sue and was to use as a guiding principle when she founded BACUP was that it is possible to share experiences and feelings about your illness which are quite different from the facts which you may know intellectually. Cancer patients, she realized, had 'been there'; they had been to a place unimaginable to those who have not made that journey. Patients understood things and could talk to each other and acquire information that the doctors and nurses were not even aware existed. In Sue's company, sharing the same miseries and fears but also the small everyday triumphs of getting better, Vicky was able to relax and lose her inhibitions. She could laugh at herself; she could also cry.

'I think I've changed as a person since I've been ill,' she wrote to Alison in a long letter after she returned home. 'I'm more emotional – I cry on an open ward with no qualms now and I think I must have hardened, but I can only see things as right or wrong towards what I feel is just and right, even if I am misguided. There is little else I can do from my sickbed except to influence others' lives for the good and I am not ashamed that I do it to my utmost.'

At the time she was only thinking of her immediate family and friends. She had been working steadily through the list of thirty-six objectives and she refuted any suggestions, from David in particular, that she was being manipulative. However, these words have a prophetic ring for the future.

Vicky was learning to be a patient. Her relationship with Sue had shown her that sharing a common experience in adversity created a bond and provided immense solace. She made other friends on the ward. An older woman told Vicky how she had devised a very effective night-time hair net out of her old tights – a solution which Vicky was to try out for herself and pass on as a 'tip' in due course to others. She loved the idea that patients could help each other in practical ways. She was also very pleased if she could help them with information. She realized that they were no different from her in that they, and often their relatives too, wanted to know what was going on, and why, if only to retain some measure of control over their lives.

As one who was both doctor and patient she threw herself across the divide that separates the two sides, offering herself as a bridge of communication, something she was to develop to a quite remarkable degree when BACUP was in its stride. But at this early stage she only knew that she 'needed to hear information repeatedly before it would sink in'. However, her medical training did at least enable her to know what questions to ask and, almost as important, how to ask them. It made her realize how much more difficult it must be for people with no medical background to understand the often complicated reasons for a particular procedure, especially when conveyed in language so abstruse as almost to be a foreign tongue.

According to Sue, at least in those early days, Vicky did not completely throw off the mantle of doctor. She was very happy to advise and she was always very willing to help anyone who asked her to explain what they had just heard from their doctor or a nurse. If she could not elucidate everything she would probably suggest further questions they could ask but, with the exception of Sue, she always kept a certain distance between her and the other person. For instance, the woman who had lain in the bed next to Vicky during and after the hysterectomy, did not know what cancer she had had until after her death, when she asked Dr Slevin. She was amazed to learn that it had been the same as hers, cancer of the ovaries.

Although in time to come Vicky would speak extremely frankly about her cancer and what her illness had meant to her, often to strangers or to large groups of people – to the world indeed through her many media interviews and her own writing – there was, nonetheless, an innermost core of herself that very few people were allowed to know. Those that were thus privileged knew another person – much more reflective and inward-centred than appeared in the normal, everyday contact with her as, for instance, those who knew her as a colleague or, in later times, as a boss.

In this, as in so many other ways, Vicky was a fascinating paradox. She was reticent about her own feelings; she was, in particular, very concerned not to let people know about the extent of her physical pain and suffering. In view of what she did go through later in her illness, her fortitude was quite extraordinary. Only those closest to her, the nurses and doctors who tended her and her very dear and near ones, knew the full depths she plumbed.

This operation made her feel as if she had been kicked by a horse. The pain was acute, seemingly endless, night and day, and she wrote to Alison that she had taken 116 distalgesics in twelve days – 'no meagre sum!' It was typical of Vicky to record this detail even though she was feeling so terrible at the time. True to form, if complications were possible, Vicky would have them. On this occasion it was her stitches which caused trouble; she also had a much more severe reaction to the chemotherapy than previously.

If all this were not bad enough, she was suddenly overcome by severe depression. Maurice had warned her that this was a very likely reaction but Vicky had not really heard what he was saying. It took her by surprise and the rational Vicky, who always tried to find a reason for everything, could not understand why it was happening to her now. She had, after all, defied the medical prognosis. She had survived three months. She had endured the chemotherapy and it had worked. The cancer had shrunk sufficiently for the operation to be possible and it had been pronounced a success. Why then, was she feeling so awful?

The plunge in hormone levels following the hysterectomy

would have been a contributing factor, but it was not so simple as that. When Maurice Slevin had laid out the odds for her at their first meeting in August, he had made it clear that she had no more than a one in five chance of success. For Vicky, that had been more than enough. She had known with total certainty that she would be in the twenty per cent survival category. Now Maurice had upped the odds of cure to fifty per cent but *only* after a further three months of chemotherapy.

Untypically for Vicky, she had a failure of nerve. Others, including her doctor, Maurice Slevin, who had always been concerned about her euphoria, saw it as welcome evidence of realism impinging at last. Whatever the reason, suddenly these odds seemed to her to be very bad indeed. To have gone through so much, and now to have to face more misery, with the possibility at the end of it all that she would fall into the unlucky fifty per cent! It was, she wrote in her diary, 'a bitter pill to swallow . . . realize Beecher's Brook over and others to come . . . [it] frightens me to end with the prospect of continued ill health for maybe two or three years and then to die!'

Tim, her ever loyal supporter, at first felt angry for her. It was as if the victory, once only a dim possibility, had become a promise which must be fulfilled. But, as David, and even Vicky, when she had had time to think more about it, pointed out to him, the truth was that it was a miracle she had got so far and this was something they had always known deep in their hearts. They had accepted in August that the months ahead would be difficult and uncertain – how difficult only Vicky could comprehend after she had been through the ordeal. From the outset they had deliberately chosen the path of cheerful optimism, in part because that was always their way of tackling any problem, large or small; in part, it was a form of self-protection, or what is now described in psychological studies as 'positive denial.'

There was nothing false about this determination to bolster their own spirits by maintaining a positive forward-looking stance before the world. It was absolutely in character for both of them and, as Vicky herself wrote in her diary on 13th December, the day after she came home from hospital: 'we would never have got through the task at hand ie 3 chemotherapy and laparatomy without it – and in convincing others there was hope we fanned our own flames of hope greater than what we should have ever hoped for.' It was an attitude that was to carry them through even more taxing trials and tribulations in the years to follow.

From time to time in her life, in earlier days when she was in good health as much as during her illness, Vicky would take stock of where she was at, usually by recourse to a diary or in a letter. Now, back at home after her worst bout of illness yet, she sat down and wrote out her feelings in simple, terse language. Halfway through she made a note to herself that she would ask Tim to photocopy the pages so that she could enclose them with her next letter to Alison. This she wrote on the following day – 14th December – and it is this letter which has been quoted several times already in this chapter. Its tone is quite different from those she had written earlier. It conveys a buoyant yet somehow much more considered, realistic state of mind. She started it:

'I've been to hell and back over the last 10 days – dragging Tim and David with me too – but I'm sure it's all been important and a worthwhile phase to go through – a growth point as they say. I want to send you my diary as I want you to "be there" with me as Tim and David have been and share in my despair and come up with me with my optimism.'

One of the sorrows for Vicky in these months had been her distance from Alison. They had had many long transatlantic telephone conversations but these could not quite make up for the times when she would have loved to see Alison at her bedside and share with her then and there the things that were happening to her and the thoughts she was having.

Vicky was right. Her cancer had changed her as a person. It had not turned her into someone different but it had developed latent qualities that were waiting for the stimulus that would make them flower as we shall see later in this book. She had discovered that despite her medical training and former clinical experience of treating cancer patients, she was as vulnerable as anyone else when it came to dealing with her own illness. She too had been prey to irrational feelings and terrifying mood swings; hopes and fears and anger; above all, a sense of desperation that her life was running out of control.

'Who would have thought I would ever have said I was happy to have cancer?' she asked herself in the diary in the middle of a passage describing her fear of the future. Her meaning is not altogether clear but it seems from the context that she is referring to the past which now seemed in retrospect so much less bad than that which was awaiting her.

In the opinion of Sue, 'this cancer thing really brought her out'. Others were to make observations in a similar vein, especially later on when Vicky was in the throes of creating and then running BACUP. But now in mid-December 1982, feeling battered and exhausted but very relieved to be home, all she could really concentrate on was preparing herself for survival. Somehow, she would fight her way through that next round of chemotherapy, knowing that she was risking herself in a venture the outcome of which was quite unpredictable.

Medical experience of the treatment was still very limited. She and Sue were only two out of ninety patients with ovarian cancer who were receiving it as part of a trial and it had not been going long enough for people to be able to notch up time markers. Five years was far over the horizon.

In her diary she compared herself to a shipwrecked person

who, having been rescued by someone with a dinghy containing food and water, paddles for hundreds of miles, braving shoals and currents and storms. Eventually she is washed up on shore only to 'realize you're on edge of Sahara desert and hope of rescue slim at best'.

The best bit of news for Vicky in those days just before Christmas was that Tim had decided to forgo for the time being his ambition to stand for parliament as a Liberal candidate. They both felt that with so much uncertainty surrounding Vicky's future he simply could not afford to spend so much time away from her side. Vicky had told him that she wanted to get the most out of being at home, and she wanted to share those pleasures with him. They had always made their decisions together and this one was no different. She appreciated the sacrifice he was making for her but, as she wrote in her diary: 'If I die or live, Tim can always go back to being a PPC – for the next election!!' Meanwhile, they could be happy together.

A few days later it seemed as if she might die quite soon. She had been feeling steadily more ill as the run-up to Christmas started. Shopping, visitors – including her father who always induced a certain dread – and the general pre-Christmas hysteria made her think that she was just overdoing it. In fact, she had developed septicaemia and on 22nd December, the day before her birthday, she was admitted into Barts, this time into the Annie Zunz cancer ward. Christmas passed in a feverish blur. Outside it was very cold and snowing. She heard the carol singers in the square below and thought she must have gone to heaven.

A week later, weak but regaining her friskiness, she was ET again, pleading to be allowed home. That night she had her postponed Christmas dinner and the next day she woke at seven o'clock, 'very excited and starving'. They were going to the cottage where they would celebrate the New Year with

Tina and her children. They sang on the way, made a fire on arrival, ate soup and turkey and settled down to an evening of video films, going to bed at two-fifteen in the morning. No wonder that the next day she was exhausted, spending most of it in bed playing monopoly with her niece, Dominique. She decided not to see the New Year in but she was happier than she had been for a long time.

Who could tell what 1983 would bring? Whatever her fate, Vicky was eager to be launched upon it.

7

Across the Desert

❖

VICKY WAS AS well prepared as anyone could be for
what lay ahead. She knew how reduced and low the
chemotherapy would make her feel; she knew too that
it would be all worth while if it meant the cancer could be
finally eradicated. Already it seemed to be on the retreat. Her
natural optimism was beginning to reassert itself. And then
there was this special treat she had been planning with Tim
since before Christmas – a holiday in Morocco.

They arranged the dates to fit in between her first and
second course of chemotherapy so they flew to Marrakesh
after she came out of hospital at the end of January. They
stayed in the palatial Mamounia Hotel where their bedroom
looked out towards the magnificent pink-tinged Atlas mountains. Vicky basked in the hotel's luxury and its air of Moorish
fantasy embellished with Victorian touches. She particularly
enjoyed having breakfast served to them on their balcony
with a flourish, the table covered with a fine damask cloth and
grapefruit cradled in tall silver goblets.

Although she was weak from the chemotherapy, Vicky
managed to swim several times in the heated swimming pool
and her shaven head and swift sliding through the water
earned her the name of 'Newt' from Tim. She walked once or
twice into the town and they bought a carpet in the *souk* for
the cottage. She was even able to manage a few excursions,

the most thrilling being a car drive into the Atlas mountains. She returned to grey, wintry England feeling revived and strengthened for the next bout of chemotherapy.

At the end of March she had her third laparatomy. The cancer appeared to have gone completely. Scrupulous as ever, the surgeon, John Shepherd, took thirty biopsies of which only three showed microscopic signs of disease. After much discussion with Maurice and Tim, Vicky decided she would have an 'insurance policy' of a powerful single shot of chemotherapy. This would be administered directly to the bone marrow and would require very careful management because it lowers the blood count dramatically, thus increasing the risk of dangerous infection. It would mean a three- to four-week stay in hospital.

Meanwhile, Vicky had been observing some new and rather worrying side effects of the chemotherapy. She was getting symptoms of peripheral neuropathy with numbness and tingling in her fingers and toes. This is a delayed side effect of cisplatinum, the most potent of the drugs she had been ingesting in her monthly 'cocktail' of chemotherapy. As is quite normal, it was appearing after she had finished the regimen. This unpleasant and disabling side effect is usually at its peak two months after the final dose before it slowly starts to disappear.

On 25th April, a lovely sunny day when she was up and about, feeling 'reasonable' for the first time for about a month, she decided to list her medical experiences, observing: 'if this illness doesn't make me a better doctor – I don't know what will.'

The numbness in her fingers made it difficult for her to write, turn taps and door handles, break eggs, sew on buttons, dial telephone numbers and put on her eye makeup. Her fingers felt stiff and she noticed wasting in the fourth and fifth ones on both hands. Almost worst of all for her was that she was aware that she was finding it increasingly difficult to play the piano. Whereas three weeks earlier she had been fatigued after playing two pages, now she was weak from the outset and she was finding it hard even to do quite simple runs.

Her feet were also giving her trouble. She found it hard to walk up and down the stairs and she was unsteady, even toppling over when she was washing her face in the hand basin. Her shoes, she wrote, felt peculiar without elucidating precisely how. The tingling sensation persisted even when she was at rest which she found particularly wearing.

Altogether the recovery from this second course of chemotherapy and third operation was proving much more painful and long drawn out than she had anticipated. In addition to the peripheral neuropathy, she had been suffering acute colicky pains for weeks which the painkillers did not seem able to bring under control.

Most of May she felt miserable and depressed by her invalid condition. When, she wondered, was she ever going to feel better? In view of all these problems, it is amazing that she could contemplate further, even more toxic medication especially as it was so high risk. But this was typical of Vicky. Anything going in the way of medical intervention which might be beneficial, she wanted. Despite everything, her diary records outings and treats snatched with David whenever she felt even slightly perky (a favourite Vicky word). She went on a clothes buying spree, the first for a year, and visited the Chelsea Flower Show. Gardening had become a passion for her and some of her happiest diary entries record planting bulbs and window boxes and sowing seeds. She bought herself a typewriter and taught herself basic two-finger typing so that she could write her letters and continue her work on her thesis. She also started driving again.

On 31st May she had to go into Barts to have a Hickman line put in under local anaesthetic, in preparation for all the medication she was about to receive. This is now a common procedure which involves putting a small plastic line into a vein under the collarbone to enable blood to be taken or fed in and injections and various medicines also to be absorbed. In essence it is a convenient form of drip for anyone undergoing a considerable amount of medication and it is inserted under local anaesthetic. None the less, Vicky found it a stressful experience, especially as the site where the line had been inserted continued to be sore for some days.

On 7th June she went back into the Annie Zunz ward in Barts for her hot shot of high dose cyclophosphamide. The night before, when she had seen what the regimen involved, she wrote in her diary: 'looks horrific . . . I am frightened'. Vicky was never daunted in her quest for complete information about everything being done to her, even though her medical knowledge made her appreciate in a way ordinary patients often cannot, the full extent of what she was letting herself in for.

On Thursday, two days later, it was the General Election, a lost day for Vicky, but on the Friday she was able to record that she had woken up to hear that it had been a runaway victory for the Conservatives. Tim, of course, had been very involved in these political events. The early part of the year had been a busy time for him; he had been hammering out policies with his Liberal colleagues in order to frame an Alliance manifesto with the SDP in readiness for the Election. Now he was dividing his time between his demanding job, Liberal meetings and the hospital.

By Sunday, 12th June Vicky was at home and able to enjoy a family lunch with her two sisters and mother, even though she described herself as feeling 'like poisoned mouse in garden', a reference to one she had found a few days earlier. On Tuesday, she organized a celebration supper for Alison and Michael who were finally home from America. The cooking was shared between her mother and a temporary cook who, Vicky had already decided, must go just as soon as she was feeling a little better.

On Wednesday, 15th June, Tim drove her to the Hackney Hospital (a branch of Barts) where she would have to stay for the next few weeks under very careful supervision to monitor her reaction to the cyclophosphamide she had had ten days earlier. It was the tennis season at Wimbledon so whenever she felt up to it she would watch the matches and then comment on them in her diary. On Sunday, 3rd July, the day of the men's finals when John McInroe won the singles title for the second time, she met for the first time the hospital chaplain, an American called Doug Hiza, and discovered to her pleasure that he was a former professional tennis player. She recorded in her diary that they had a 'marvellous chat re CA, death etc. and tennis'.

Vicky and Doug were to become very good friends over the next few years, as she was to be a frequent inmate of the Hamilton-Fairley ward, then in the old Hackney Hospital and later in the new Homerton Hospital. They would have many talks on many subjects. God was not one of them. 'It's not something I push,' Doug Hiza told me. 'I talk about what patients want to talk about.' Nor does he remember talking about death very much either to Vicky. 'Vicky talked much more about life. She had such a terrific zest for life. We also shared a lot of ideas and mutual concerns.'

He warmed to her enthusiastic, outgoing personality, finding her American rather more than British or Oriental in this respect. Vicky found him equally sympathetic because he was ready to share her excitement and interests, particularly in communication, and later, when the concept of BACUP was beginning to take shape, she would bounce ideas off him. There were, of course, times when he would see Vicky in quiet, reflective mood. 'She was down but not unhappy.' He felt it was a natural and necessary way of working through her grief. 'Those quiet times when she was being introspective, she was taking an inventory, looking at her life.'

The day after she met Doug Hiza she was given the all-clear from Maurice and so, at the end of a beautiful summer day, Tim drove her home to Clapham. 'Hot, and so lovely to be back,' she wrote in her diary. 'Walk round garden slowly – supper in bed – David visits and sits in garden with Tim 'til 11 saying how great I am getting over this!'

They were right. Her survival was a triumph. It was almost a year since her cancer diagnosis and in those eleven months her small frame had endured major surgery three times and several massive onslaughts of toxic drugs, all with the aim of driving out this wretched disease. Bald, battered and tottery – her feet were still very uncomfortable – she was none the less alive. Very much so and burning to get back into the swing of things.

Within days of getting home she was picking up with renewed vigour her writing of an important chapter for a medical book which summarized the original research she had been doing on opioid peptides in human beings (basically the role of acupuncture in pain relief). She was also ringing estate agents for David who thought he needed a bigger house; she was 'popping into' Peter Jones to buy garden furniture for the cottage; she was making iced coffee and cleaning the kitchen floor; she was lunching with her mother at the Selfridge hotel and buying a hat; she was picnicking with David at Sissinghurst – 'Vicky Clematis Jones!'; and she was arranging a holiday for Tim and herself in Italy, booking hotels and flights.

Her energy was astounding. It was leaving her fit friends gasping, and somewhat alarmed. David, she noted one evening, was 'quiet, low re transition ill to well ... vacuum now I'm better.' He had already talked to her when she was still in hospital about her work, advising her to take it more easily. Alison, her close friend who knew from old how absorbed Vicky could become in whatever she was doing to the exclusion of caring properly for herself, said the same. Maurice Slevin was in agreement and, as her doctor, went so far as to suggest that she should not think of extending herself until 1985 but then, he did not know Vicky at that time as well as the others did.

Vicky began to worry about herself just a fraction when she saw how the old tensions of juggling work with the demands of home life and her relationships were beginning to creep back. On 17th July, only a fortnight after she had come home from the hospital, she noted: 'I feel I am riding headlong into well health – too fast, must stop. Must change my life. So happy when ill – as time for Tim and David – decide to be General Physician.' But the next day she was in Barts, ostensibly to have her Hickman line removed but it was also a good opportunity to visit friends and colleagues. She basked in their approval and admiration. Everyone was genuinely surprised and delighted to see her looking so well and her boss, Professor Michael Besser, said, as she noted in her diary: "'You look great; when are you coming back to us?" – typical!' To Maurice Slevin she gave a stethoscope, an expression of her gratitude to him for having saved her life. Both she and Tim were in no doubt about that.

She had ten days left before the end of the month when they were due to leave for Italy. She wanted to finish the chapter and she felt under pressure to meet the publisher's deadline. A normally healthy person finds work in these circumstances stressful. For someone in Vicky's state of health it must have been exhausting but she persisted in her usual way, verging on the manic. She noticed one day that her foot was slapping down noisily on the floor, so, at Maurice's insistence, the next day visited a neurologist in Barts who diagnosed a combination of neuropathy and popliteal palsy. The palsy is caused by pressure on the popliteal nerve in the foot and can happen to office workers who spend long hours with a leg pressed up against a desk. The following day Vicky continued to work hard on the chapter but no longer crossed her legs as she thought this might be causing the foot drop. She was writing sections of her chapter and delivering them to the typist right up to the day before they finally took the plane to Italy.

The Italian holiday was a great success, even though, quite predictably, Vicky was exhausted for the first few days that they spent in Bellagio on Lake Como. It was a time for Vicky and Tim to be alone together and enjoy each other's company. Nothing and no one to think about but themselves. How they needed this time! They had been through so much and the support Tim had given Vicky had been unflagging. She could not have survived without it, as well she knew, but now he needed to recuperate just as she did.

Day by day Vicky grew stronger and they were able to do a few excursions, visiting some of the villas in the area with their beautiful gardens. One evening she was noting in her diary that she could only walk about 'very, very slowly'; yet the very next day she was playing table tennis. She bought a pair of Adidas trainers which she wore for the first time in San Gimignano and noted with approval that she was 'walking well – footdrop appears recovered!'

For the second half of their holiday they had driven south to Siena in Tuscany, stopping overnight in Bologna. In Siena they stayed in 'La Certosa', the beautiful converted monastery and Vicky loved every moment. By the end of the week she had seen and done more than most tourists attempt in twice the time; she had visited museums, galleries and churches and taken one or two trips further afield.

Tuscany in the height of summer is not a restful haven for the tourist who is culturally inclined; exploring the hilltop towns with their narrow cobbled alleyways and steep steps requires determination, if not stamina. Vicky had the first in abundance even if illness had temporarily deprived her of the latter.

Vicky was brimming with energy – both physical and mental – and was always ready to tackle anything but she was also clever at husbanding her resources. In healthy times she would not have seen the point of losing breath climbing an excessively steep hill when she could be using that same breath much more profitably to expound her ideas. All the same, whatever the condition of the terrain, she would still have covered it very fast, as she always did. In sickness she was not going to allow her fatigue to deprive her of beautiful sights she had travelled a long way to view or, in other circumstances, to cut short her opportunities of talking with friends and others whose opinions she valued.

When Vicky's physical energies sank low she would summon up her mental ones to take over and propel her to achieve whatever task she had in hand. It is not surprising that many people asked to describe how they remember Vicky, come out first with the simple word – Energy.

A friend observed with some amazement, like many others who came into contact with Vicky at this time in her life, that this extraordinary energy continued, despite the advance of her illness. He recalled a much later occasion in Vicky's life when, on a visit to their home in Upstate New York, she got it into her head that she wanted to learn how to play baseball, having just been much impressed by Robert Redford's way with a bat in the film *The Natural*. This was not Vicky expressing idle curiosity. Once an outstanding athlete herself, she genuinely wanted to know about the game. What is more, she wanted to play it. There then ensued, in his words, 'a somewhat bizarre game of baseball on a tennis court'.

*

72

No sooner landed in England on Friday, 12th August and back home in Clapham, than Vicky unpacked and did her accounts. She also recorded that she now weighed seven stone and eleven pounds. The following days were full of bustle and activity. She was up and down to the cottage, visiting David, sorting out her correspondence, tidying the house, polishing, cleaning and cooking.

'I am so frisky!' she reported – another typical Vicky expression – but then, as the days passed, she noticed that she was having more hot flushes for which she took some medication. She wondered if anaemia could explain her fatigue. A hint of depression creeps into the entries – 'a bit miserable – this is ridiculous – should be happy, still alive!' she wrote on 16th August. A week later she was organizing her trip to Lourdes, undertaken at the behest of her father and made only to please him. It was not an experience she enjoyed or from which she derived any comfort. It is probably significant that there are no diary entries covering this period.

At midnight on Friday, 30th September Vicky was lying awake, tossing with pain from a new infection. Shingles had attacked her three days earlier and it was making her feel sorrier for herself than at any time she could remember. So bad was it that she was driven to get up and address a quite lengthy homily to herself, on paper, about the fatuousness of these feelings, given how much she had come through already. The pain, she told herself, was as nothing compared to what she had suffered with her other illnesses – all listed – but her despair was deep and it frightened her.

She writes poignantly: 'I wish I could have energy again and run!' One can imagine her looking out of her window into the night, the beautiful garden – largely her creation – exhaling its languorous autumnal scents below her. Did she remember the fifteen-year-old Vicky, lithe and vibrant, running down the track ... away from her rivals ... so fast, faster than anyone?

She wondered whether she had been overworking in the past few weeks. Certainly, she had been having sleepless nights about the prospect of treating patients again. She had also worked excessively hard on her chapter in the previous days, even when measured by Vicky's standards, in order to complete it before returning to work on the following Monday. Did it mean her health was not compatible with a normal working life, normal at least for Vicky? Would she ever fully recover her strength and vitality?

In those lonely hours she asked herself these and other more disturbing questions about her state of mind, writing them down in an effort to crystallize the essence of what was troubling her. This was a practice she was to repeat at frequent intervals throughout that autumn and the record reveals an unhappy and deeply depressed Vicky.

It was no good admonishing herself: 'Every morning I should think Positive ... My negativeness is no help to anyone – let alone me. It may give chance for tumour to grow again – I'm the one who said it right at the beginning that positive thinking may boost immune system!!' She felt empty and useless. She was worried that she was frightened by the prospect of returning to work. Her memory was not so good as it had been. She felt inadequate and out of her depth when talking to her colleagues. Quite absurdly, in view of how exceptionally hard Vicky had always worked, she was now feeling 'like a drone on society and that I have never done a day's work'. Although she knew such sentiments were irrational they were quite beyond her control. They engulfed her and they absorbed her every waking moment.

She was appalled that after all her struggles to keep alive she could find no joy in the prospect. She found herself staring into space and being tempted by the thought that it would be so 'nice and easy just to be dead'. Why was it so difficult, she asked herself, to make the transition from being ill to well? She answered her own question: 'it's really easy being ill – people don't expect anything of you – no pressures – a copout – you just make people happy by being easy, not complaining and being understanding. Once you are a bit better and start doing things e.g. work – writing and having less time, people can't understand why you no longer have all the time in the world to speak to them and concentrate on their worries!'

Immediately she reproached herself for having such ungrateful thoughts. After all, it was not just she, Vicky, who had struggled. Those closest to her – Tim, David, Alison, her family, her doctors – they had all fought the battle with her and had suffered for her. She could not let them down now: 'it's just not enough to have been brave in illness, I should be brave in recovery and show people what I can do.' In typical Vicky fashion she immediately wrote down what she should be doing in her work: writing protocols, talking to people, doing some minor experiments. And, to round it off, she counted her blessings. She was loved, she had money and two lovely homes. Above all, she was alive. 'Now show them fight for life has been worthwhile and enjoy life while you can.'

From time to time Vicky makes these somewhat oblique references to her mortality. During that September night she had asked herself why she never thought about or even feared the possibility of recurrence – 'maybe it's the unthinkable' – but, of course, even to pose the question was to be thinking about it. Later that year, when she was plunged deep into her depression and wondering whether it might be clinical, so paralysing had it become in its effects, she dared to articulate the unthinkable but clothed it in a characteristic paradox. 'Why be so gloomy? I may be dead in 6 months – enjoy life – be cheerful – use experience of last year.'

Years later, when the cancer had recurred and she knew for

certain that it would never again go away, she was able to admit frankly to others as well as to herself that when everyone had been telling her she was well and that she could resume her life as before, it was she who found it hard to believe that she really had a future waiting for her. 'I couldn't understand why I was there, really. It's a strange, strange feeling.'

By the end of October she was feeling worse. She felt herself sinking into a morass of gloom from which she seemed unable to extricate herself but just as the muddy waters were threatening to close over her head she clutched at a branch that promised salvation. Of course, why had she not understood this before? It was her job that was causing the problem. She realized she no longer had any appetite for research. She did not want to pass her days 'rattling test tubes' and writing papers. She had always deeply disliked the political intrigues and the in-fighting that were a feature of the department in which she worked; in the past it had often upset her and indeed, she pondered in this diary, as had others close to her, whether the stress of trying to mediate in these personality conflicts, combined with overwork, had not contributed to her illness.

In earlier days the merest whiff of competition had been enough to stimulate Vicky to even more prodigious efforts; now, she was finding that the 'keen as mustard one-upmanship' of everyone from professors to registrars was 'salt in the wound'. Unexpressed but nevertheless there, lurking beneath these doubts, was the old childish fear of failure that she thought she had long since vanquished. What if her illness really had affected her mind in some way? No matter what Tim and her friends said to reassure her, for instance, that it was perfectly normal to feel unsure on re-entry after such a long rough ride, Vicky remained tormented by self-doubt and uncertainty. She felt inadequate and incompetent. She was also terrified that she was making a fool of herself and that she would bore all her friends to death with her agonizing. Vicky was not a moaner but when she had a problem she did expect her friends to help her tease out a solution in just the way she was always ready to offer her own services to them when they needed help. This meant exploring and examining in minute detail every possible option.

She kept reminding herself that having been through so much it would be ridiculous to turn into 'a Wimp and a Wet' now. She felt she wanted to do something useful with the 'second life' which had been given to her – a phrase she uses more than once. It is an echo of a conversation she had had months earlier with a colleague who had visited her in hospital and in the course of the conversation had expressed the view that if one could choose one's mortal illness, cancer was perhaps preferable to heart attack because it gave one a chance to put one's life in order. There is nothing particularly original about this idea but for some reason it struck Vicky very forcibly at the time and she often alluded to it. It gave her the key she needed to unlock that mystery which had been puzzling and paining her. It was the mystery framed by the question 'why me?' which is so often asked by cancer patients.

She had at one time wondered whether God was punishing her for some divine unknown purpose of his own. That thought had occurred to her even before she had been diagnosed with cancer and she had expressed her fear aloud to more than one friend. But if God was to be dismissed, as he was in due course, then she had to find her own sense of purpose to make her life liveable. Vicky was always intensely goal-orientated. As she explained later to Professor Anthony Clare, you would not want to wish cancer on anyone but, having had it touch her life she wanted to show with other cancer patients that 'instead of our lives being shambles we can build something from it'. What that something was to be was not yet clear in Vicky's mind but she was already stumbling and groping her way towards the vision which finally was to crystallize into BACUP.

She began to think of alternative careers: general physician, endocrinologist, oncologist, senior lecturer, consultant, or even GP. She considered them all but found herself rejecting those like endocrinology which would involve her in lab work and still more research. She was looking for something else: contact with people, an opportunity to put her experience with cancer to some practical use. Why not then be an oncologist? She had spent long enough on oncology wards to have a good idea of what it involved. It would mean a lot of research and working long and hard hours to become really imbued with the subject but she was not afraid of that. Would it make her depressed? She discussed the pros and cons of this career at length with all her close friends but it was a conversation with Maurice Slevin which was to decide her finally against this option. He told her that she was too close to her own experience to be able to cope reliably with patients, many of whom would be distressingly ill. Give it five years, he suggested, and see how you feel then. That was no good for Vicky who felt instinctively that she had no time to waste but she accepted the good sense inherent in his view.

'Patients . . . I am good with patients . . . I have got something special to give patients . . . I can be sympathetic . . . I get on with them, they get on with me . . . I feel you can psyche patients to be better . . . I can't have family now – I want to look after families.' This urgent sense of wanting to work in close contact with patients is a recurring theme in her deliberations. She rejected the idea of being a hospital consultant because she felt that this was not the best way of establishing a doctor-patient relationship. She was convinced that as a doctor who had been through a life-threatening experience, she had a unique weight of experience to offer and to share with patients which would be more accessible to them in a GP's surgery than a hospital consulting room.

The notion of working as a GP began to appeal enormously – 'being a good GP is a skill I would love to acquire'. She wondered whether she would find herself being emotionally drained by patients. Her medical friends warned that she would miss the intellectual challenges she had always enjoyed hitherto but Vicky saw in general practice an opportunity to 'free her mind'. She was tired of competition and rivalry, always trying to outsmart her peers. She thought she might be able to use the GP base to do other things – 'hospice work, cancer help, the attitude of mind, community medicine'. She was thrilled by the new horizons opening up before her.

There was too a very practical attraction attached to being a GP. It would give her more time for her private life – maybe she could even work part-time, at least at the beginning. She was firmly convinced that for the sake of her health she must do different, less taxing work. She wanted to be relieved of the need to be an expert and to put an end to the frenzied life ruled by writing papers, reading journals and meeting deadlines. She hated that nagging guilt that overcame her when she was not reading up on her subject in her spare time in the evenings and at weekends. Above all, she wanted to enjoy her life with her husband and the company of her friends; to have 'time to cook for them and time to talk to them . . . Friends really are more important than anything'.

Beneath all these declarations which fill her diary through November and into the beginning of December there lingers still the other Vicky who can write: 'While I was ill in hospital life was rather like a crusade. I would like it to be again.' And then again: 'Have to set an example to others that it's possible to be saved from brink and be useful and successful after – don't shy away from the challenge!!' Which Vicky would win out only time would tell.

By the end of the year, Vicky had crossed her desert and it seemed that rescue was there after all. Physically she was much better, no longer getting so tired and her depression had lifted. After consulting many people she had finally made up her mind. She would train to be a GP. As soon as possible in the New Year she would seek out a practice where she could be taken on as a trainee. Once again she was feeling human. On 23rd December, her thirty-fifth birthday, she wrote in her diary: 'Tearful on waking – still alive after one year!'

It was not the first time in her life that Vicky had had to adapt her life to changing circumstances.

8

Growing Up in East Grinstead

❖

(1957–1967)

FROM HONG KONG to East Grinstead ... from the thronging streets of an oriental city to the stodgy respectability of Home Counties suburbia in the mid-Fifties ... spicy noodles to fish fingers. In the six short weeks that it took their ship to transport them across the world, the lives of the Yip children had been utterly transformed.

Tina remembers the eight-year-old Vicky sitting on top of the furniture crates in the empty house and prising them open, one after another, with a hammer. Vicky remembered herself feeling sad because she had had to say goodbye to all the new friends she had made on the voyage. 'I was crying and singing some songs, wishing I was back on the boat – that safe place where I'd felt really loved for the first time.'

The Yips arrived at their new home at the end of August 1957. The house was a detached four-bedroomed brick villa with fenced garden behind and a tidy tarmac parking area in front. Brand-new, it was on an estate being developed as part of East Grinstead's postwar expansion into a dormitory town for London.

Betty remembers a day when she came running back to the house in tears after being teased unmercifully by the other children because she was Chinese. Vicky was at home doing her homework. 'Tell me who they are,' she said. 'I will sort these kids out.' And she did, laying into them with fisticuffs.

They were taken aback by this diminutive Chinese girl defending her sister so vigorously and slunk away. It had been hard for Vicky, too, in the early days but she had learned how to cope with the bullies. Withering scorn was her first line of attack but if that was not enough she was not afraid to use physical force. What she lacked in strength she more than made up for in nimble dexterity.

England was the first place where the Yip children encountered racial prejudice. It came as a great shock and it began from the day of their arrival in East Grinstead when local children came up to their house and started throwing stones at the windows, chanting, 'Ching, Chong, Chinaman'. Susie had no hesitation in taking on her neighbours. She went round to all their houses, rang the door bells and said to the occupants, 'We're new here, like everyone else. This is our home. Please treat us properly.'

In those days they were the only Chinese family in East Grinstead and there were few if any social conventions about concealing your racial prejudices. In that narrow, buttoned-up milieu the Yips would have been regarded as thoroughly outlandish, the more so because there seemed to be no man about the place.

They had arrived just in time for Susie to buy their uniforms and get them ready for the start of the new school year. She sent Tina, George and Vicky to the nearby Notre Dame Convent school. George who did not enjoy his time with the nuns moved swiftly on, first to the East Grinstead Grammar school and then, after doing his Common Entrance exam, to Dover College as a boarder.

With George, her rival, removed from her immediate orbit, it might have seemed that Vicky could take life a little more easily. But that was never her way. She told a friend many years later that she found those early months in England very hard, mainly because of the language problems and the strangeness of the people and the surroundings. The playground gibes hurt and she felt humiliated in front of her new-found friends. They threatened her first opportunity to establish herself as a person in her own right, independent of the family from which she was struggling, subconsciously, to free herself. She wrote later in her life: 'I remember how painful it was sometimes when I used to forget that I was different, and then some small incident would cruelly jerk me back to reality. After the rudeness I resolved to show everyone that, despite my race, I was as good if not better than they were. Thus my achievement drive was even further developed, though I still secretly doubted my abilities.'

Poor Vicky! This inferiority complex was a burden she was to find great difficulty in shedding. It is quite possible she might not have achieved all that she did, had she not been so driven by the need to disprove her imagined inadequacy.

The nuns were anxious to keep Vicky, their star pupil, and offered her a free place but Susie decided she would do better at the grammar school. Her daughter, the doctor-to-be, must not be handicapped in any way from achieving her mother's ambition. This move marked the real start of Vicky's integration into the English way of life and culture but it was never to be complete. There would always be a little bit of Vicky deep inside that kept her an outsider in her adopted country despite the education, the achievements and the marriage. One school friend sums up what everyone else who knew Vicky in those days, teachers included, has said about her: 'She was so good at everything and so nice with it. She did it so effortlessly and with such talent that we never felt jealous of her.'

She sounds almost too good to be true, an Angela Brazil heroine who is not only the most popular girl in the school but is also the prettiest, the cleverest, the nicest; and, to cap it all, shoots the winning goal or saves the school from some disaster. Vicky's only disappointment, voiced to me twenty years later, was that she did not achieve being head girl.

Otherwise it was all true. Vicky could and did do everything, and a bit more besides. She was a scholar who regularly scored marks in the nineties. She was a very talented musician, playing the guitar (which she taught herself) and the violin as well as the piano in which she attained Grade VIII level. As an athlete she was exceptional, winning several sprint records and playing hockey for the county. Her place on the forward line was inner right where she was 'quite lethal' according to a friend. Pauline, the daughter of a footballer friend of Teddy's who came to live with the Yips in East Grinstead for several years and was especially close to Vicky, remembers telling her once, 'You look like you want to kill the person in front of you when you are running,' to which Vicky's simple answer was: 'I probably do.'

The school photograph of 1964 with its massed ranks of boys on one side and girls on the other, shows Vicky standing amidst her friends with head held high, straight-backed and smiling confidently into the camera, every inch an English schoolgirl, albeit with an oriental slant of the eyes. She wore her black hair shoulder length and although everyone admired her and liked her, she was well known for not being a flirt. Even if she had wanted to be one, which she did not, she would not have had much chance because Susie was very strict with her two older daughters. They were not allowed boyfriends, parties or discos.

Although Vicky appeared to do everything so easily, in reality all her achievements were backed by sustained effort. 'Quiet, methodical and studious' is how she is remembered by one classmate. These were characteristics which she had developed from early school days and they were to stand her in good stead as she worked her way through school, university and medical school. Pauline remembers in particular

Vicky's remarkable ability to concentrate on the task in hand and shut out the world around her.

One evening Pauline cut her finger so badly that they had to ask a neighbour to drive her to hospital for treatment. When they returned, Vicky, who had continued studying throughout the uproar, looked up from her books in genuine surprise to ask where they had been. Pauline does not remember feeling hurt by her apparent indifference — just admiration that she could be so totally absorbed in what she was doing. Vicky was also kind and patient. She taught Pauline to ride a bicycle and read in English and always had time to spare to help her with her homework. As the children grew older Susie would leave them more often with 'Auntie', a relative of Teddy who had taken over from the nurse. After Tina left home Vicky was responsible for the household management and she would do many of the chores — shopping, cleaning and mowing the lawn. Pauline still uses her as a point of reference today. 'When someone says, "you can't do everything," I have to say, "but I know someone who could and did".'

The teenage Vicky was outwardly an eager, enthusiastic joiner, a keen Guide, a girl with 'a great giggle' and someone who was always willing to take her part in the team; inside there was a private Vicky who shrank from revealing herself. She was vulnerable and shy, very conscious of the fact that her home life was rather different from her friends. One of them says they guessed that Vicky had secrets she could not talk about. 'She never talked about her father and we never saw him but we knew she was frightened of him. I always had the impression that she kept out of his way as much as possible. They didn't have a family life like we know it. People weren't invited back very much. I never felt I knew Vicky all the way through. She never let on that she was angry or upset. She'd never argue with you or have a row. She would just walk away, switch off. She used to get exasperated with lesser mortals who were not on her wave length but she would never be rude or hurtful. You could never really get to know quite what Vicky was feeling.'

Pauline, who was Vicky's most intimate friend at that period of her life, did have a fairly good idea of her innermost feelings. 'A lot of the time Vicky felt very insecure and fragile but she would only reveal that when she was caught off guard. She was far more sensitive than she would let on. She felt that her parents didn't love her and it became a vicious circle because the more she put on this harsh appearance of not caring, the more, in a way, she rejected their affection.'

Whatever Teddy's feelings about his second daughter, and they were certainly complicated, of Susie's love there can be no question. She was always there for Vicky's big events: the concerts, the hockey matches and the piano competitions. She did all the things caring parents do for their children but she was, to all intents and purposes, a single parent. For many years she had to run the household finances on a tight budget. When George was at Dover College she would save up out of the housekeeping for the train trip and when he came back for the holidays he would be the one to distribute the pocket money and dole out in equal portions the tinned peaches or other special treats.

Teddy visited his family twice a year and never stayed for longer than a week. 'It was like a black cloud waiting for him,' said Betty. 'It hung over us while he was there, and it was a wonderful relief when he went.'

On one occasion he was out walking on a dark wintry morning. Unexpectedly, Vicky emerged out of the gloom on her bicycle and told him she was doing a newspaper round. When Teddy told the story many years later, he was smiling broadly, so it is possible that he congratulated his daughter on her enterprise; it was just the kind of thing he would have done. Scoldings, and worse, were more often the order of the day.

George remembers his father encouraging the competition between him and Vicky. He used to make them run races and once Vicky beat her brother, much to George's chagrin. She also loved playing football with George and his friends and this did meet with Teddy's approval. In every way Vicky tried so hard to be the son he wished he had had instead of her. It was an endeavour she carried on to the end of her life. Eventually he was able to say openly that he was proud of her – after she had died – but then he added, and this too was totally in character, that she was a chip off the old block.

In truth, Vicky did have many of her father's qualities. She had inherited his dynamism and energy, his capacity for quick thinking, his decisiveness and his musical gifts. Teddy was a gifted singer and loved improvising on the piano and the guitar. The ruthlessness and single-minded determination to achieve her ends which Vicky was to show later in life were also reminiscent of Teddy. To some degree also she shared his obsessive compulsions, though she was always very worried that they might teeter into the full-blown manic depression from which he suffered. What she did not share in the slightest degree was his ill-controlled temper which would explode into irrational outbursts and frightening displays of violence. Vicky did get angry but only very occasionally and afterwards she would feel miserable about it. Usually it was on someone else's behalf rather than for herself.

Her father's irregular appearances in a clap of thunder and her mother's difficulty in getting accepted into local society made it impossible to establish an English-style family life. Susie's grass widow status and her good looks made her an object of suspicion to neighbouring wives which she was never able to overcome entirely. Vicky regretted that they did not enjoy the humdrum cosiness her friends took for granted.

They, on the other hand, envied her the trips abroad – to Hong Kong and Paris where Teddy had an interest in a Chinese restaurant – and the exotic aura that surrounded the Yip family.

Despite these diversions Vicky's mind was always on her studies. She wanted to go to Cambridge and read medicine. George had been accepted to read law at Magdalen College. If he could do it, so could she. She had, after all, proved that she was his intellectual equal when, spurred on by his example, she had passed the intelligence tests to become a member of Mensa. Vicky believed that she was disadvantaged by her grammar school education and the headmaster was discouraging. He told Susie that the school was not geared to Oxbridge entrants and that his teachers would not be able to coach Vicky adequately.

Nothing daunted, Vicky offered herself for a place at Cambridge in the last term of the Upper VI. She was turned down. This was a terrible blow. Vicky was not used to failure; she hated and feared it but she felt she must rise to the challenge so she insisted on trying again. Encouraged by her good A-level results and the support of one teacher, she stayed on for another term in the VI form, unheard of at that school. To her great joy she was accepted for Girton. A new life was waiting for her.

9

Bright Light

❖

(1968–1982)

VICKY AND ALISON had kept in touch since their first meeting at their Girton interview. On that occasion Vicky's brother George, who had already been up at Cambridge for a year, invited them to tea in his rooms. He served them muffins and treated them with avuncular condescension. They were tremendously impressed by the surroundings and Alison particularly marvelled at George's *sangfroid* and apparent total integration into Cambridge life. As he showed them round his college and explained its history he seemed more like a don than an undergraduate. Alison envied Vicky her good fortune in having this assured entrée into university life.

Their first rooms in Girton were on opposite sides of the college. Vicky had a tiny room on the orchard side while Alison occupied what she termed a garret on the library side. She remembers Vicky having a cupboard filled to overflowing with tins of food and crockery. As she came to know Vicky better, she realized that this was very typical of her; she liked to be prepared for any eventuality.

In her first week as a fresher Vicky met the man in whose company she was to spend most of the rest of her life. She was nineteen. He was eighteen. First impressions were not auspicious. It was the Trinity 'coming-up' ball and Tim was drunk. They were introduced by a cousin of Tim who was also a school friend of Alison. Tim was not too drunk to remember that Vicky, despite her shyness, made the running. She told him all about herself and her life and was delighted to discover that his family home was so close to hers. He lived in Haywards Heath.

The next day the two girls acted on Tim's invitation to visit him in his rooms for morning coffee and there was embarrassment all round when they discovered that he was still in his dressing gown. The unpromising start was quickly overcome and it was not long before Vicky and Tim were recognized as a couple. Every Sunday she cooked lunch for him in her room and they spent as much free time together as they could muster.

Vicky was given George's dashing red MGB when his father gave him an Alfa Romeo. She was thrilled. A fast confident driver who could double declutch with aplomb – a skill she had been taught by Teddy – she would whizz round Cambridge from lectures to piano lessons to parties and, some weekends, she and Tim would fling their bags into the back and drive up to London.

Vicky had brains, money and an exotic image. Tim had the confidence and easy manners of his family background which she admired and wanted to make her own. In character they were very similar and were to grow more alike as the years went by. 'Tim and I are enthusiasts' was a phrase Vicky was to say often about themselves and it was absolutely true. They were also both great believers in working for a cause. In later years the lawyer and the doctor were to live that ideal to the full in their lives but, no matter how great the pressure, they always managed to preserve their taste for a healthy dash of hedonism.

Vicky embarked on her new social life with great gusto. An early triumph was to be chosen as the symbol for the Mandarin Ball; she was also the runner up to the Rag Queen. She played hockey for Cambridge and won a half blue. For a while she joined the sporty set and became secretary for the Polo Club, going to some of the same parties as Prince Charles who was in George's year. She and Tim went to all the balls.

Vicky played hard. She worked even harder. The stakes were higher and the competition keener than any she had experienced hitherto. Cambridge was bulging with people quite as bright as her so getting to the top was going to be no pushover. Her school friends do not remember Vicky ever being overtly competitive. That all changed at Cambridge. She became very single-minded about her work and extremely competitive – with Alison who was equally keen – and every-one else.

Medical students have one of the heaviest timetables to handle. Vicky and Alison did nothing to lighten their load. Lectures started at nine o'clock every day including Saturday. They never missed one. Practicals took place in the afternoon and often there were tutorials in the evening. They used to study for hours at a stretch, taking copious notes of everything. The two girls had become very close friends so they always sat together at lectures. They were also keen rivals so they made a pact with each other that one would not study without the other, thus gaining an unfair advantage. They were insepar-able to the point that one could not even go to the library on her own, although Vicky confessed many years later to another friend that she did find this obligation rather onerous at times. In their second year they shared a room and when they were preparing for their exams would stop only for breaks or melted cheese on Ryvita or fruitcake.

'People thought we were gay,' said Alison, 'but it was just that we found each other fascinating. Male medics seemed very grey and boring to us. We spent those three years, talking all the time about everything.'

Vicky was never a feminist in spite of all those occasions in her earlier life when her father's powerful presence might have made her feel sympathetically inclined to the cause. Indeed then and in later years it sometimes seemed as if she did not really like women very much, apart from those favoured few with whom she made deep friendships. She certainly had little sense of solidarity with her sex. Vicky was perhaps too Chinese for that. She could never forget her position in the family and the way girls and women were regarded as of no account in the Chinese culture. She reacted in a typically Vicky way.

Her response to any hint of sex discrimination was a robust 'join 'em and beat 'em . . . soundly'. This was an attitude which would become more entrenched as she pursued her medical career. It would serve her well in achieving her goals in the supremely male-centred world of medicine but it did not always endear her to women she encountered on the way.

One woman who first met Vicky as a medical student, disliked her quite intensely for slightly different reasons in those days, although later they were to become very good friends. Pamela was a stunningly beautiful model who was engaged to one of Tim's friends. She realized Vicky had little interest in her because she had no pretensions to be an intellectual and made it obvious she had no wish to join in their noisy, argumentative debates.

'I thought Vicky was very unfeminine. She was driven by ambition and she was so influenced by her father. She didn't care about women because she was driven by this need to prove herself and men were the competition, so only men counted.' Pamela's relationship with Vicky changed quite dramatically when several years later Pamela became pregnant with twins and Vicky invited her to stay with her and Tim during her pregnancy. A completely different Vicky was revealed.

'I had never known before that she had a fun side to her. She was so warm and so concerned about my babies and incredibly supportive. She became family. She was also so wonderful in the house. She'd be at work all day, then cook these gourmet meals, then play some Chopin nocturnes and then work all night. The atmosphere was incredible.'

Pamela grew to love Vicky dearly and their relationship was based on a deep mutual appreciation and affection as well as the shared pleasures of shopping and decorating and cooking. Pamela, though older, felt that she brought out the mother in Vicky. When she had personal problems Vicky was always ready to offer her much-needed solace and wise advice. With Pamela she could be the prop and resource that she loved to be for her friends. Pamela is, however, realistic about the basic reason for their successful relationship. 'It was the lack of competition that made it easy for us to be friends.'

Vicky became considerably more self-centred as she tuned into Cambridge life and discovered just how much there was to do and learn. Her family noticed the change in her. When she came home she would no longer so readily offer to help with the household chores or show interest in what was happening in their lives. She was entranced by the world she had discovered and the wide horizons that were opening up to her and she was determined not to lose any opportunity for taking full advantage of what was on offer to her.

She had always been very adept at organizing her daily schedule so that she could pack as much as possible into her life; this now became a skill refined to a fine pitch of perfection. Vicky never wasted an instant. Her mother remembers her walking into the house on the first day of the vacation, having driven over from Cambridge, with her first piano pupil waiting for her. She would book them in so that she could start teaching the moment she arrived and lose no time between lessons. This ability to use her time profitably was combined with a very keen sense of priorities. Vicky never wasted either thinking or physical time on what she had decided were inessentials. It was a skill which was to stand her in good stead throughout her life.

One after another, she picked off the glittering prizes. She won a Girton College exhibition and the Pheiffer graduate scholarship; she also won the Elizabeth Walton prize and the Raemaker's prize, both from Girton College. Best of all she achieved a double first: in her Part I Medical Sciences Tripos and in her Part II Archaeology and Anthropology. She and Alison chose this latter course as an alternative to doing a further year in pre-clinical medicine and it was a revelation for both of them. Instead of learning everything off by heart they were at last studying in the real university sense: they were reading critically, acquiring knowledge for its own sake rather than for some ulterior vocational reason, and they were plunging deep into debates about ideas and theories.

'A bright light' is the way Vicky's former headmistress recalled her. Vicky was a very direct person; in some ways she was simple to the point of naïveté. She was far too intelligent not to realize fairly early on in her career that she was cleverer than most people so it would have seemed dishonest to her to pretend to be less than she was. She certainly did not suffer from any twinges of false modesty but equally, she disdained bragging. Only when she felt it would be useful did she talk about her achievements as, for instance, when she was setting up BACUP and needed to establish her credibility with important people.

'Vicky was one of the most humble people I have ever known,' said Jenny, a new friend who came into Vicky's life soon after she had come down from Cambridge. 'I never knew she had won any prizes and the only reason I knew she must be good was that everywhere she went people always wanted to keep her. It was quite a shock when I heard Anthony Clare talking about her brilliant career.'

Jenny first met Vicky and Alison when she advertised for flatmates to share her Pimlico flat. Alison arrived before Vicky and appeared to know exactly what she wanted. When Vicky turned up later, she seemed by contrast to be rather quiet and retiring. Vicky was now doing her clinical training at St Thomas' Hospital while Alison was at the Middlesex. She did not particularly enjoy those three years because she found her fellow students, most of them male and several of whom she had known at Cambridge, rather stuffy. She also felt uneasy with the rigid, hierarchical system but it did give her a kick to discover, quite by chance, that her mother's father, Ho Sai Kwong, had also been a medical student at St Thomas. He never completed his studies because his family ordered his immediate return when they heard that he was going out with an English girl. Although they were Eurasians they disapproved of marriage outside the Hong Kong network so they 'lured him back', according to Vicky, by sending him a picture of her beautiful grandmother-to-be, Flora.

In July 1974 Vicky was doing her first house job at the Lambeth Hospital. It was now that her friendship with David blossomed. Recently returned from Vietnam, he too was enjoying the practice of everyday clinical medicine, preferring to care for patients in a total way rather than pursuing a specialty or becoming involved in a particular area of research. He encouraged Vicky's interest in general medicine and she began to realize how much she enjoyed the work and that it was an area where she could really shine. She loved the close involvement with people and the feeling that she was helping them. She gained a reputation for extraordinary thoroughness in taking notes and finding out all she could about her patients. The consultants for whom she worked during that period were very impressed by her. Her star quality earned her the pick of the London house officer jobs, enabling her to follow the so-called 'golden trail' which culminated in October 1976 with the offer of a coveted post as rotating registrar in Medicine at Barts. She had passed her Part I membership exams for the Royal College of Physicians earlier that year and in December she passed her Part II. Now she was all set to start her career proper in medicine.

When Vicky and Tim came down from Cambridge in 1971 they decided they would be sensible and not get married straight away. Apart from one fairly short separation between their second and third year when Tim at least had felt boxed in by the relationship, they had been together all the time. They felt they should give each other some space now while Tim worked for his Law Society exams and Vicky completed her medical training. Although they lived in separate flats they still saw each other several times a week. In the event they married a year earlier than planned because they realized they would have much less time together once Vicky qualified and started on her house jobs. On 16th June 1973 Vicky Veronica exchanged vows with Timothy Francis and gladly changed her name from Yip to Clement-Jones. They were married at the Roman Catholic Church of St Thomas More in Upper Cheyne Row, Chelsea, and Vicky combined traditional Eastern and European styles in her lace veil and long cream-coloured wedding dress with a mandarin collar. There was a reception afterwards and the whole affair was as conventional, in the upper-class mould, as anyone could wish for. Vicky, always a stickler for doing things correctly and in the best of taste, was well pleased.

They moved to a flat on the south side of Clapham Common and settled down to married life. Tim joined the Liberal party that year and immediately became very involved with local politics. They used to meet frequently with Alison, David and other friends for long evenings passed in lively discussions over the dinner table. Vicky enjoyed cooking and could produce wonderful meals for special occasions. Her pleasure in food dated from her earliest years when her mother took her shopping in the streets and alleys near their Hong Kong flat.

Vicky would have seen from her pram the heaped mounds of glistening *suchus* (sweets) in one shop, gleaming roast ducks impaled on long poles or salt flecked dried fish in another; and the pavement stalls piled high with tempting delicacies — sugar cane, *mawlaw bows* which are bread rolls made with a sweet dough and every kind of delicious *dim sum*, those titbits both sweet and savoury which the Chinese will eat at any time of day or night. Vicky never lost her taste for Chinese food but she also enjoyed experimenting with other cuisines. One of her greatest pleasures was to find a new restaurant and share the discovery with friends.

David remembers the first time he was invited to join them for one of these meals. 'They all knew each other very well and they were used to shouting each other down. I listened for a while and then I realized that the only way to enjoy myself was to pitch in. So suddenly I banged the table very loudly and said: "Now listen to what I think . . ."'

It was in these years that David and Vicky forged their special relationship through their love of music. Vicky had discovered a piano in the common room at Lambeth Hospital and when David revealed that he used to play, she persuaded him to join her in a duet. Their different personalities blended very harmoniously in their playing: Vicky, always so project-orientated, sharpened and improved David's execution. He, on the other hand, as a reflective person who was more interested in the 'why' and the 'how' of things, the process rather than the end product, mellowed and deepened her interpretation.

A regular time for playing would be on Sunday mornings in David's house after Vicky had already done probably a couple of hours work at home or in the hospital. Then she would return home and cook Sunday lunch for Tim and herself. Occasionally she and David were asked to give a public performance. David remembers one occasion when he and Vicky were sitting at the piano, waiting to start. He was so nervous that his knees were literally knocking together and she admonished him, saying quite crossly: 'Stop that! You're shaking the stool.' Her scorn had the desired effect. It banished his stage fright.

Although both she and Tim were now working very hard they still gave themselves time to take exciting foreign holidays, a pleasure to which they had grown accustomed during the long summer vacs at Cambridge. Money was no longer a serious problem once they were both earning but Vicky never became a big spender — on herself at least. She was renowned for her generosity to her friends and would choose presents for them with great care but, where she was concerned, she preferred to save and have money in the bank.

Her relationship with both her parents had changed quite remarkably. For her mother she was more like a sister and confidante than a daughter. Her father would seek her advice on any medical matters and started to treat her as his favourite child. She felt that he still did not really love her enough but she was proud that she had succeeded in winning his respect because of her achievements.

Vicky's reputation had preceded her at Barts and before the end of her year on the training programme, Professor Mike Besser, head of the department of endocrinology, had offered her a research fellowship in his team. It was an offer too good to refuse and it was in an area of medicine that Vicky found very interesting.

She arrived at an exciting time. The department was just then at the beginning of researching into naturally occurring opioid peptides in the brain tissue — endorphins and enkephalins — which it was believed could be harnessed to act as pain relievers. They had recently developed an assay (measurement test) for one of them and now needed to do the same for another one called met-enkephalin. Professor Besser suggested that Vicky should have a go.

Without further ado she settled into the laboratory and under the guidance of senior colleagues worked incredibly hard to produce an assay. Before the year was out she had achieved this goal, indeed she produced the world's first specific assay for this compound. She then proceeded to study its mechanism as a pain reliever. Her research led her into contact and later collaboration with a Hong Kong neurologist called Dr Wen who had been investigating the effects of acupuncture on heroin addicts.

Three years after she had joined the department she was awarded a fellowship from the Medical Research Council and appointed an honorary lecturer with senior registrar status. In 1980 papers appeared in both *The Lancet* and *Nature* in which, as lead author, she described the research which led her to establish, among other things, that there was a physiological link between acupuncture and pain relief. A flurry of other papers written by her, together with other members of the department, and relating to various aspects of her work, appeared in a number of scientific journals at around the same time. They were followed up by invitations from various learned societies to give papers at several international congresses.

This brief summary of Vicky's achievements in those six action-packed years at Barts hardly does justice to the sheer volume of work that she put in, neither does it reflect the extraordinary energy and enthusiasm with which she addressed herself to every task. Her colleagues remember her with a mixture of awe and delight.

First of all her appearance. She would arrive for work on her Honda two-stroke motor bike, a slight figure in an orange motor cycle jacket, rain-proof trousers and a white-peaked helmet which, when doffed, revealed a pretty young 'girl' – she was then in her late twenties – who looked so different from the conventional medical stereotype no one at first could quite fathom who she was. She was always on the move, darting from laboratories to offices to wards in the sprawling Barts complex.

Professor Besser expected his registrars to combine their research with clinical medicine so that they could accrue the necessary accreditations to become consultants. In Vicky's case this meant that on top of a more than full-time research schedule which made very rigorous intellectual demands on her, she was also looking after patients with exactly the same degree of empathetic attention that she had given them in her previous posts. Being Vicky, she put 100 per cent plus into everything she did. She was persevering and painstakingly thorough to the point of obsessiveness. She set herself extremely high standards of performance so, quite naturally as it would have seemed to her, she expected the same pitch of perfection from her colleagues and others who worked for her. Her energy was seemingly inexhaustible.

Vicky was saved from being an insufferable prig, despite this daunting profile of excellence, by her sense of humour and her genuine caring concern for others, particularly patients. Her uninhibited enthusiasm was also very infectious. One of her colleagues recalls: 'She would get very excited about the latest result and come and bang on my door and say, "you must come and see this." You couldn't resist her.' Another describes her as 'one of those rare experiences you have in life. She was exactly the sort of person you need to keep you on your mettle.' Vicky had found a cause: she had an opportunity to push forward the frontiers of science just a fraction and she wanted to share her excitement and her discoveries with anyone who was interested.

There was, however, a problem. Not everyone was as fair-minded as she was. Almost for the first time in her life she experienced the devastating cut and thrust of academic politics. For the most part the swords were clashing above her head but there was one incident which concerned her personally and caused her deep distress. In 1982, after all the remarkable work she had done, some of it original, she was certain that she would be offered a senior post that had become vacant in the department. She was not and she was very angry. It was one of those rare occasions in Vicky's life when she expressed her anger openly. She was made even more bitter when it came to her notice that there were hints that she had tried to buy her way into the job. This was because her mother had given a generous donation for a new laboratory. Vicky, who hated conflict and rows, suddenly found herself at the centre of a storm, and it upset her greatly.

It disturbed her to see what people would do for the sake of political advantage and, even worse, that such base motives could be imputed to her. The experience, though deeply painful, was not entirely without its uses. From it she learnt one or two political lessons which she would have no scruples about putting to good use later when she was running BACUP. However, some of her friends still wonder today whether the stress she then experienced over a prolonged period may not have contributed to her illness.

It is a question that has no answer but one thing is certain: Vicky may have been good at looking after others but she took no care at all for her own health. She was working all hours, eating junk food a lot of the time and frequently skipping meals altogether. Tim remembers her even at Cambridge lying on the floor groaning and twisting with acute stomach cramps. Her brother George says that she often complained of severe stomach pains which she would diagnose as hunger. It is certainly strange that when her cancer was diagnosed it should have been at such an advanced stage. Vicky and Tim were both convinced that it was probably present at the earlier crisis when she was rushed into hospital with acute peritonitis but that it was unsuspected and unseen because of the pelvic abscess.

Again this can be no more than speculation and Vicky, true to character, always thought it an utter waste of time to indulge in reminiscence or regrets. What was done was done. It was important to get on with life today, not think about the past.

10

Second Life

❖

VICKY STARTED THE new year of 1984 with a typical flourish. She decided on nothing less than reorganizing the whole house from top to bottom. Her illness for most of the past three years meant that piles of stuff had accumulated which until now she had had neither strength nor inclination to weed out. Clearing the house would be both a symbolic and practical declaration of intent. It was a celebration to mark the end of her depression and it was a preparation for what she had determined was to be her 'second life'.

On New Year's day she began in her bedroom, clearing out cupboards and throwing out a 'huge amount of jumble and clothes'. She moved down to the dining room where she installed an art deco lamp she had just bought and from there she went to the large airy basement kitchen where she cleared out more cupboards, re-arranging the contents to suit her after the months that other people had been using them. She made a New Year's resolution to cook Chinese and did so that very evening: she and Tim had a quiet TV supper by the fire of fried chicken, cauliflower and prawns. The following day was a Monday but still a holiday so she finished off the dining room and then started on the study. This was a really big undertaking because Vicky was a great hoarder.

Tim called her 'an intellectual squirrel'. She kept everything, treasuring her mementoes from childhood on. She stored them mostly in plastic bags but also somewhat haphazardly in files which were rarely disturbed. School reports, exercise books, account books, every single draft of every paper she ever wrote, diaries which she kept off and on throughout her life but sustained steadily from 1981 when she had rheumatic fever – her first serious illness – letters, theatre programmes, and anything else that might be deemed of any significance at all – at least to Vicky herself – were kept. In this tendency to hoard Vicky was certainly her father's daughter.

Teddy Yip has two offices in Hong Kong: one is a magnificent but hardly ever used showplace commanding a splendid view over Hong Kong Harbour and situated high in the Shun Tak tower which straddles the Macau ferry – one of his many business interests; the other is a dusty, cramped two-roomed bolt hole in an anonymous building on Des Voeux Road Central. Here the leather chairs are shabby and sagging and you have to dislodge piles of magazines and files to find a place to sit. Plastic bags are on every inch of flat surface and piled on top of each other. The carpet is distinctly grubby, the beige walls are covered with photographs of the Great Man, his Formula One racing cars and his motor-racing pals. There are very few family pictures: one is of Susie, who looks out of the frame, meltingly beautiful with large almond slanted eyes and softly curling shoulder-length hair. She has written a loving inscription to Teddy and the picture was probably taken at much the same age – nineteen – as Vicky was when she was going up to Cambridge. Another is of Vicky herself, the picture that is on the front cover of this book.

In spite of the three factotums (two of them male) and the endlessly ringing telephones you would be hard put to imagine that this office belonged to one of Hong Kong's wealthiest tycoons of whom it is said that one out of every four grains of rice eaten in Hong Kong are imported by his company. Teddy's lack of ostentation as regards his office quarters suggests prudence rather than any lack of self-esteem. Why spend money on a place where he spends as little time as possible, he would argue, and why advertise your wealth unnecessarily, especially when there are so many better ways of spending money?

In her home surroundings Vicky liked to be surrounded by nice things – antique furniture, original paintings, carpets and other decorative pieces that she and Tim had picked up on their travels – but in some ways she shared her father's propensity to be frugal. She was, for instance, never a big spender on herself, preferring to save and to keep a tally on what she had in the bank. She kept careful, up-to-date accounts, no matter how ill she felt. Susie, her mother, remembers how as a child Vicky was always looking for ways of making money. The newspaper round was continued for some years; she would also go fruit-picking and do anything else that she could fit in between all her other activities. The piano lessons continued long after she really needed the extra money any more.

She was equally as good at saving money for other people. When Susie won several thousand dollars in a Las Vegas casino during a family holiday, Vicky immediately found an American Express office and suggested to her mother that she buy traveller's cheques with her winnings so that she would not fritter them away. Susie took her advice and then spent all the money over the next few years on presents for her children and grandchildren.

Vicky combined her personal thriftiness with unobtrusive generosity to her husband and her friends. It was a quality she had always had in abundance even as a child when, according to her brother George, Vicky was always the first among the five children to share out whatever she had – in those days it was never very much. It was a generosity that she showed in much more than gifts. She was ungrudging with the amount of listening time she allowed to her patients; she would share her ideas and discoveries freely with her colleagues; and she would be ready to spend hours on the telephone with a friend who was seeking her help or stay up into the small hours to discuss another's pressing problem.

Vicky's generosity of spirit was a quality she took with her in abundance into her second life but as time went on it would manifest itself differently. There were some in her intimate circle who would find it hard to accept that they were no longer first on the receiving line for what was to become her most precious commodity – time. But all that was yet to come.

At the end of that Monday, 2nd January 1984, Vicky felt quite exhausted. She and Tim had spent most of the day sorting and stacking medical journals and papers. She sprained her wrist but she did not allow that to prevent her doing her accounts. Christmas had been one of the best ever. They had had a marvellous time surrounded by family and friends. Tina and her children had come to stay; Betty had cooked the Christmas lunch at her home in East Grinstead. On Boxing day she and Tim had gone down to the cottage and Alison and Michael with their toddler son had come to stay. No sooner had they gone than other friends arrived with their children; David came on the 28th and so it went on – a house full of happy family parties and a steady stream of sociability ending with a New Year's Eve party in London given by Alison and Michael. At the cottage they had eaten salmon and ham and parsnip soup and bread and butter pudding and 'delicious fish pie in pastry', all cooked by Vicky. It had been a prodigious effort but she had enjoyed every moment of it.

Vicky was back at work in the laboratory at Barts on Tuesday, 3rd January but her wrist was giving her trouble so the following day she had it X-rayed. It was put in plaster for a suspected fracture which meant that temporarily she could not carry on with her sampling and 'test tube rattling' in the laboratory. Never one to waste a moment, she took advantage of the unexpected free time to ring around some GPs in her South London neighbourhood whose names had been given to her by David because they had expressed an interest in taking her on as a trainee. She fixed appointments with about half a dozen to meet them and sit in on their surgery sessions during the following week which she did, diligently, although by the end of the week she was back in the lab as well, 'fiddling around' as she put it with some complicated assays.

She wrote up notes after each of her GP visits, observing the doctor's manner and approach to his patients and the kind of practice he ran. She began to ask herself, as indeed friends had already, whether she would be able to stand the humdrum routine and the form-filling which seemed to take up so much of a GP's day. There seemed to be no time to get to the bottom of anything or really communicate with the patients. She realized that many of the people in the doctor's surgery were presenting with social rather than physical problems and she thought that her helplessness to alleviate their hopelessness might make her quite left wing but also depress her. She felt that it was all rather overwhelming, even a little frightening and she wondered whether she would miss the safer, because more structured, environment of the hospital where she knew she belonged and had a recognized position in the hierarchy.

She compared the disadvantages of general practice with the ones she wanted to leave behind in her hospital life: the pace, the competition and the finicky tedium of so much of the research work she was doing. It was marvellous to achieve results and recognition but Vicky had become heartily sick of this particular road to success. She saw it as paved with what had become for her 'mindless' laboratory procedures and hours of private time spent reading, referencing and writing up her work in faultless detail. And yet, it was still necessary to ask herself this crucial question: 'How important is this feeling of being somebody, and known and recognized as such?' The answer would come in due course.

Tim, with whom she discussed all these questions at length, was firmly convinced that she should leave hospital medicine. He felt that she was unsuited temperamentally for the ruthless power politics that all too often, unfortunately, appear to be essential in medicine for climbing the ladder. Furthermore, he was very concerned that a perfectionist like Vicky, who now felt pressurized because she had so much work to catch up on due to her three years of illness, might once more be over-stressed and become ill again. Most telling of all, as far as he was concerned, was the fact that she no longer enjoyed the work.

'What is INTELLECTUALLY STIMULATING anyway?' she wrote in her long self-examination on Sunday, 8th January. 'As long as I can feel I'm doing a good job and have self respect in relation to it then I should remain happy.'

It had been a lovely day. She had had coffee with David in the morning and unburdened some of her angst about becoming a GP. She was pleased with the rug she had bought for the kitchen. After lunch with Tim and a quiet afternoon, no doubt passed in more discussion on the same subject, she had attended a concert at the Wigmore Hall with two musician friends. Now, after supper and a hot bath, she was sitting at her typewriter mulling over her various GP experiences.

Vicky wanted to practise 'humane medicine', by which she meant caring for patients in a compassionate, sensitive way. She felt she had seen enough of the environment in which a GP has to work, especially in a run-down inner city area, to realize how difficult it was to achieve a good patient-doctor relationship. Perhaps, she acknowledged to herself, she had idealized it beyond its practical realization, or possibly, in general practice, it ought to be seen as a service rather than a relationship. Would it, therefore, be easier in a different version of the hospital setting which she knew so well? Perhaps she could combine all the things she was good at: communicating with patients and caring for them, while at the same time doing some interesting research and possibly teaching others to learn these skills from her. She imagined herself running 'an unusual sort of ward with greater emphasis on the doctor patient relationship'.

In the process of analysing her reactions Vicky was led to formulate the type of work and medical care she really wanted to explore in her second life. She drew up what amounts to a six-point agenda for action which, if she had lived, she would undoubtedly have completed. In the event she achieved much of it but the special significance of the proposals she typed that Sunday evening on a single sheet of A4 paper is that they clearly show the direction in which Vicky was moving. A support organization for cancer patients was not yet even a gleam in her eye but the frame of mind embedding these proposals, which follow here in a paraphrased version, was to become the bedrock philosophy of BACUP.

There were four avenues of inquiry Vicky wanted to explore. First, does a positive attitude alter the outcome of illness, cancer in particular? And, related to that question, can counselling influence such attitudes? Second, is there a relationship between stress and illness? Third, is honesty about diagnosis and treatment important to patients, whether in relation to cancer or any other serious disease? Fourth, could complementary therapies like relaxation and meditation or just the fact of finding pleasure in some activity (as she did with the piano) be an aid to recovery?

Unbeknownst to her at the time, Vicky, in expressing these concerns, was lightly touching some new notes on the keyboard of medical awareness. It was in the mid-Eighties that doctors finally began to accept that there are many cancer patients – probably the majority – who have pressing psycho-social needs and problems every whit as serious as their physical ones. The evidence had been there for years, staring at them out of the unhappy faces they saw on their daily ward rounds and in their clinics but, because it was articulated mainly by patients and relatives in the form of anecdotal statements, it had been disregarded as inadmissible and therefore unproven. Now at last there were some cracks emerging in the armour of medical complacency; a few research studies were being set up here and there, perhaps because there were just too many patients complaining about the way doctors patronized them and lied to them.

Honesty was the quality Vicky believed to be the most important contribution doctors could bring to their relationship with their patients – and it was the one too often signally deficient. First-class researcher that she was, she noted the need to produce 'some data that honesty benefits patients and their families' because, she writes, 'if one could change the profession's attitudes and practices in this respect and in relation to terminal care that would really be an achievement'.

The rest of Vicky's story is a testament to her outstanding success in achieving this ideal of truth. Unhappily, there are still many sad stories of medical lies and evasions reported by patients to the BACUP nurses but at the same time there are many more doctors who accept that patients have the right to know the truth if they ask for it. Although Vicky did not have time to pursue the research she knew was necessary to substantiate her intuitive hunches about the relationship between stress and cancer and the value of complementary medicine, she would be glad to know that others are now following her lead.

Points five and six on her agenda were more immediately action-orientated. She resolved she would learn about terminal care, possibly by working in a hospice, so that she could then 'apply those skills to a home context or even [to] wards in a general hospital where dying is still such a distressing affair for patients, relatives, nurses and doctors'. Vicky knew what she was talking about. She had seen death on the ward, in her previous life as a doctor, and now as a patient. She had witnessed the pain, the bewilderment and the anger suffered by so many people and it had upset her very much. She remembered with some sadness that she herself, when a doctor, and acting from the best of motives, had sometimes denied patients the dignity of preparing for their own death. That must not happen any more, nor would it if she had anything to do with it.

Her second and most immediate action, she determined, would be to join a cancer support group, either outside the hospital or one linked to an oncology unit, such as the one her own doctor, Maurice Slevin, ran from the Homerton Hospital. 'I should get a lot of buzz out of this,' she writes, 'helping to dispel taboos and being half way between fellow patient AND DOCTOR.'

There was another point on this agenda but it comes tacked on at the end: it was not so much an afterthought as a subconscious indication that these other concerns were beginning to take precedence in her mind. '. . . Finally general practice itself: how one can affect people's lives, help them, practise preventative medicine and by positive attitudes help them to get better and stay well.' Only a day later, when Vicky came back to her notes she was asking herself: 'am I being realistic that I could do the kind of extra work that I envisage and be able to achieve anything and be satisfied by it?' The BACUP seed had been planted but it was buried deep in a frozen winter soil and it had not yet even germinated.

By the time she had concluded her visits at the end of that following week her mind was made up. She had chosen the general practice she wanted to join. In fact, there were two but she hoped, with some juggling of dates, to be able to fit them both in for the year's training she needed to qualify. The first, run by a Cambridge contemporary of hers and described by her in detail, offered 'a Rolls Royce service' to both patients and trainees which attracted her because, 'the feeling of excellence would make me feel positive and good about general practice'. The second was a far less ritzy practice serving a predominately working-class area but the doctors, who were also much older, were very concerned to offer their patients emotional and social support as well as medical treatment. They were 'more feely' was the way Vicky put it which is what she wanted to become herself.

So here she was again, on a Sunday evening a week later, after a snowy weekend down at the cottage, writing her GP application forms. She was back in the lab on Monday, 18th January and worked frantically through that week but found time to organize a new yellow filing cabinet in her study at home and get all the necessary hospital references from her previous houseman jobs to back up her applications. If accepted, she would start her traineeship in September so she proposed to leave Barts at the end of June.

Now she was ready to break the news to her bosses. On 25th January, after stopping off at David's surgery to have a nerve-calming cup of coffee with him, she spoke first to a senior colleague, Professor Lesley Rees, who greeted her decision very sympathetically. As Vicky commented later in her diary: 'conversation . . . obviously struck a chord – she said she often looked at what she did and what it was all for – and I more than anyone else had "life" and that will end'. What the conversation did for Vicky was to bring home to her that mortal she might be but that need not stop her from taking the opportunity now to live a second life. It was never too late to change, no matter what the future might hold in store for her.

Her meeting with Professor Besser was equally encouraging. He too, like Lesley Rees, was delighted for her that she had decided to make this change of career although he was very sorry to lose one of his brightest stars. But he had seen it coming long ago. Both he and Lesley Rees urged Vicky to finish her MD thesis which had for so long been hanging over her. Its completion would symbolize the ending of a chapter in her life and formally release her to start the new one.

Professor Besser had another concern. He was anxious that Vicky should not be swept away by the near-manic euphoria that had seized her after the initial diagnosis of cancer in August 1982. He wanted her to be absolutely happy about her proposed change of career and certain that it was based on a considered decision. He also advised her to proceed slowly with her plans for working in a hospice and training as a cancer counsellor. He warned her that to be properly effective with others she would need time to distance herself from her own experience of cancer.

Vicky listened to him and took his warning to heart. It was much what Maurice had said to her a year earlier when she had been thinking of becoming an oncologist. She was able to reassure him that the idea of becoming a GP had been with her for some time and that she had been discussing it exhaustively with her husband and close friends for the past three months. It was only now, after she had made all the necessary investigations and confirmed that it was a practical possibility, that she was ready to announce her decision and go ahead with it.

As for becoming too swiftly and heavily involved with cancer care, again she heeded his advice, recording in her diary: 'I must remember do not be too manic or zealous about wanting to do ca counselling and terminal care – first may be too early to do it – also people may not take me seriously if too manic.' Vicky always feared this tendency in herself to go over the top. She knew from personal experience of life with father just what destructive havoc a full-blown manic depressive personality could wreak on those unlucky enough to be in close contact. In her case, her extraordinary energy was invariably powered by the desire to achieve good in some form but, even so, its effects could be overwhelming for those within her immediate orbit.

She was enormously relieved to have dealt with the difficult business of announcing her intentions. Her resignation had been accepted with good grace and she felt elated and freed 'from all that grind and feeling of negativeness about keeping up to become Endocrinologist, Physician or research at old high level'. Her diary zings with details about happy domestic activities both in London and at the cottage, meals out and conversations with friends. Several times she remarks on how happy she feels and how well she and Tim are getting on.

Tim had also had a change of career during this early part of 1984 and this was probably one of the reasons for their sense of mutual wellbeing. He had left London Weekend Television to join Grand Metropolitan for a better job with more pay. He had also become a member of the Liberal Party's National Executive.

Meanwhile the work continued to be as demanding as ever. Soon, despite often recording how tired she felt, it was as if she had never been away from the lab and she was working at her former fever pitch. In the middle of February she had a bad fright. After an upsetting family row she was gripped by severe abdominal pains and she was terrified that these might be signalling a return of the cancer. Fortunately, they abated without her having to take any further action.

She had now put in train all the formal arrangements for her GP traineeship and began casting about in her mind as to what she would do next. At the end of February she went to Maurice's Monday morning clinic for one of her regular check-ups and they discussed support groups. The idea of joining one had been on her mind for a long time, indeed ever since that black September night six months earlier when she had wondered why she should even bother to go on living. She had read a magazine article about CancerLink, an organization which supports and coordinates a country-wide network of cancer patient groups, and made a note to herself that she should write for more information. Her conversation with Maurice proved very constructive. He suggested that she join the group run by his patients on the Gordon Hamilton Fairley ward of Homerton Hospital, backed up by the support of himself and two ward sisters.

As always, when Vicky was enthused by an idea she acted upon it immediately. Ten days later she attended her first meeting at Hackney and two weeks after that she spoke to the Pitcairn ward group at Barts (all gynaecological patients) about her experience of ovarian cancer. She described it as a 'really great first meeting' and Maurice told her she was 'terrific at it' so she went home very happy. Typical Vicky! Where most people would have found one group more than enough to meet their needs, she had joined three by the end of March. The third was in Newbury which had been started in memory of an eighteen-year-old girl who had recently died from ovarian cancer and this, too, she attended assiduously.

At all three, Vicky was far from being a token presence. Although she had never previously thought of herself as a leader, now she found herself naturally taking that role and her enthusiasm was infectious. 'She was like an electric current going through the rest of us,' said Sister Jenny Ellwood, who was one of the nurses who had set up the group at the Homerton Hospital and was to come to know Vicky very well when she nursed her through the later stages of her illness.

Vicky had, of course, not joined any of the groups just for herself. She wanted to hear of other people's experiences with cancer, and learn from them. As far as her own experiences were concerned she was happy to share them and to impart whatever information, medical or otherwise, that she felt could be helpful. It was at these meetings that she became more than ever confirmed in her view that cancer patients, the people who had 'been there', had something quite unique and special to offer each other. And it was not just the patients but their families and friends who needed help and support too. Their involvement was crucial. Vicky was profoundly convinced of this because she knew just how valuable her own support system was to her. She could not have coped without it; indeed, she believed she could not have struggled back from the brink over which she had nearly plunged to the triumphant peak of survival where she now was, had not her family and friends been there throughout her ordeal, sustaining her in every way possible.

Spring was stirring and Vicky was feeling marvellous after 'a wonderful ten days holiday' which she had spent mostly at the cottage but, during that time, as she recorded on 14th March, she had also written a chemotherapy protocol, spent a day at St Christopher's Hospice, attended two cancer groups and a meeting at the Royal Society of Medicine on hypnosis, and started writing a paper on her experience of cancer. She had also organized the decoration of their London house, bought a gold chain and a new clasp for a diamond choker, arranged for a jewellery valuation and 'gardened and learnt about gardening – life can be pretty full without working!'

Later that month she went to Edinburgh for a meeting of the Endocrine Society which she found exhilarating and enjoyable. At work she was back to doing ward rounds and clinics as well as teaching medical students, in addition to her research work and writing. The diary is peppered with her *joie de vivre* – 'full of myself . . . feeling so confident and full of beans . . . tired but happy'. She was delighted to see that she was putting on weight, recording on 9th April that she was eight stone three lbs. Everything was going her way, even her racing flutters. She picked the first five horses in the Grand National, a success she was to repeat later that year by winning the first two in the Derby.

The ghosts and demons seemed to have been banished and nothing could really upset her now, not even her father's behaviour to his family which seemed to have been worse than usual in the early part of that year. Vicky had a share of her father's superstitious nature so when, in March, signs of damp had reappeared in their house, she confided her concern to her diary that this might be an omen of her own cancer recurring. She compared the trauma of installing the damp course to her chemotherapy and surgery. Great, therefore, was her relief when the builder assured her that it was of no consequence and could be easily removed. She had had one very emotional outburst returning from a weekend at the cottage spent with friends and their children when she had wept about her own 'missed family'.

It was a particularly beautiful spring that year and Vicky watched with delight as the crocuses, daffodils and tulips she had planted almost two years ago just after she had been diagnosed with cancer, appeared each in their season in her garden. She had planted them in a frenzy, the first time she had ever done such planting and quite convinced that she would never see them flower. 'The joy when I first saw them last Spring and now one further Spring on reinforces to me how lucky I am to be here and well.'

She had almost forgotten that she had ever had cancer. Apart from her numb feet and the occasional twinge of abdominal pain she felt in top-class form. 'Lovely weather, isn't it lovely to be alive.'

11

A Rather Grand Dream:
BACUP is Born

❖

TWO WEEKS LATER, on the last Saturday in May, Vicky was back in the Pitcairn ward in Barts, on a drip, feeling 'tired and awful'. What had happened?

The previous day had been one long hectic rush. She had been teaching for the first part of the morning; she then spent the rest of the day doing some very difficult work in the laboratory. This had made her late visiting a patient on the Pitcairn ward who had become a friend. From there she had raced home to change for dinner with Tim's sister and parents, hurriedly drinking a mug of sugared milk as she dressed. The stomach pains had started during the meal so she had gone home early to spend a dreadful night vomiting and taking pain killers which had no effect.

The gruelling day had come at the end of a punishing week. It had been her busiest since she had returned to work and all the signs that she was overdoing it had been there. As she lay in bed, consoling herself with her inimitable brand of optimism, that it was 'so good . . . not to forget what it's like to be ill again . . . and no longer in control,' she was also resolving that she really must learn to pace herself better. She found it bizarre to contemplate that here she was in the same ward where she had received so much treatment, the last time only nine months ago when she had had transfusions before her Italian holiday. Even odder, when she came to think about it, was the fact that it was two years almost to the day to the start of what she now realized were the symptoms of cancer. In June 1982, she had suffered an attack of acute diarrhoea just after returning from Barcelona where she had been a guest speaker, giving a paper on met-enkephalin and related peptides at the fourth meeting of the Catalan Society of Biology and the Catalan Society of Endocrinology.

False alarm! The problem this time turned out to be a minor obstruction due to adhesions developing as a result of her many operations. She was able to return home on the Monday morning, relieved and happy that it was no more serious. Nonetheless, the incident had given her an opportunity to sit back on her heels and think once more about where she was going. Yet again the sea analogy had come to mind. She thought of herself as a ship that had been sailing through a 'long storm, buffeted by [the] elements'. She had been sailing in all directions just to keep afloat but now she was into calm waters with 'sail and ship intact' and she must decide which direction to take. It might well be different from the one on which she had originally started her journey. The important thing was 'to take hold of life [now] no longer flotsam buffeted by events, treatment complications'.

She resolved she would immediately write her cancer article, 'if not a book', and that she would waste no time in finishing her thesis which she would dedicate to her doctors and all the staff who had looked after her on the three wards. A flower picture on the wall in the hospital day room where she was writing her diary reminded her how many lovely things there were to enjoy which she had discovered when she was ill. She had become a passionate gardener and she did not want to lose out on those pleasures now. Ever down to earth, she reviewed her diet and told herself that she must protect her irritable gut. Her fibre intake must be cut down; the muesli restricted to once a week; fewer apples must be consumed;

everything she ate must be chewed more thoroughly. Pressure of work had made her relapse into the old bad habits of buying convenience foods and eating at odd hours. She must be sensible and look after herself.

After a quiet first day at home, organizing her papers and paying bills, she started to write her cancer article in earnest. She found it was going well although she could not help feeling some discomfort that she was not back at work, an unease which was heightened when, on the Thursday, she took the whole day off. She drove with David to the Royal Horticultural Society's gardens in Wisley; they lunched at the Festival Hall and bought Chinese plant pots in the afternoon; and rounded off 'a memorable day' by going to hear Peggy Lee sing at the Royal Festival Hall. To assuage her sense of guilt, she went into the lab on Friday, 1st June, and after a busy weekend, socializing in London and, in the country, weeding her garden, she was back at work on Monday morning 'leaping around'.

In no time at all Vicky was working at full throttle once more, sometimes finishing as late as nine in the evening. It is not surprising that towards the end of her second week out of hospital she reports a row with Tim: he was cross with her for overworking and she accused him of spending too much time on Liberal party work. But all the while that she was racing from pillar to post and working on her usual exhaustive lab routines and procedures, an exciting new idea was churning through her head.

During this last hospital stay she had been able to talk to many of the other patients in the beds around her, several of whom had ovarian cancer and some she now knew quite well because, like her, they were members of the Pitcairn ward support group. The nurses had given her a great boost because they told her what a positive effect she was having on the group. 'I seem to say the right things at the right time.'

Vicky could see that these support groups were tremendously important to the patients. Her experience as a patient had taught her that she had the same needs as these people. She might know more about the medical aspects of her cancer, but feelings about cancer, understanding what cancer meant in personal terms and living with cancer: these were areas of being where she needed help and support just as much as the next person. Loving and wonderful though her friends and family were, some things they could not help her with, at least not to the extent that others who had 'been there', as she had 'been there', could and did.

At the same time, Vicky was keenly aware how privileged she was in relation to most other patients. Even the more articulate and self-confident among them were at a considerable disadvantage compared to her. She was a doctor, in her own hospital, being treated by her peers and, in theory, everything she wanted to know would be offered to her. In practice she knew this was not happening with other patients, not because it was being deliberately withheld, simply that it was not part of the medical stock-in-trade. The doctors and nurses who were caring for her had done their best but she knew now, from hearing other people's stories, that many health professionals were guilty of an appalling lack of imagination and sympathy.

Even her own team of carers had fallen short of the ideal, as she had learnt from bitter experience when her hair fell out after the very first course of chemotherapy. They had offered her a wig in advance but they could not prepare her for the misery of waking up every morning with hair in her mouth and eyes and the humiliation of going bald in public. They had warned her about hot flushes and a possible depression but they could not tell her how truly awful it would feel to be thirty-three – a young woman – who had lost not only her chance to have the children she wanted but was condemned to a constant reminder of her condition by having to endure many of the unpleasant symptoms of an artificial menopause.

Then, too, there were attitudes that needed to be changed: views about cancer and behaviour towards people with cancer. She knew about the fear and loneliness and anger so many patients suffered because of their disease, but often it was the ignorance and incomprehension they met in other people that caused them even more distress. She had suffered some of these cruelties herself. There had been those 'friends' who once they heard she had cancer had simply melted out of her life. Her patient friends on the ward and in the groups had told her about acquaintances crossing the road, and friends, sometimes even relatives shunning them in other situations, because they thought cancer was a 'dirty' disease or supposed it to be infectious. Cancer survivors were losing their jobs because 'You die with cancer, don't you?' Their marriages or other relationships were breaking up; people insulted them because of their strange shaven appearance; they were made to feel guilty because they had cancer – they must have a cancer personality or have lived in some reprehensible way.

The catalogue of guilt and blame that can be heaped on cancer patients is long and heavy. Vicky was shocked by the intolerable life, one almost of secret shame, that so many people were being forced to lead because of their disease. On the other hand, she was also very impressed by the courage and dignity displayed by so many of her cancer friends, even when they knew they had come to the end of their particular journey. Equally, she admired the humour and determination that drove others so often to live a normal life again: Sue, for instance, her first cancer friend whom she still saw from time to time. She was also astonished to discover just how many people there were out there in the 'real world' who had had cancer and, like her, were getting on with their lives. They were the survivors and they were doing well but, however well-adjusted they might appear, if her own experience was anything to go by, these people also needed support and recognition.

Living with cancer changes your whole perspective on life as Vicky had found out, mostly with joy and delight. There were so many small pleasures she had come to appreciate and consider as precious. She had learnt to be more reflective, 'to stand and stare and watch the flowers grow', as her friend Alison described it. The shift in emphasis can also bring devastation and heartbreak as Vicky knew full well; in her case, it was knowing she could never have children. All these aspects of cancer needed to be brought out into the open and shared with the rest of the world.

Right from the beginning of her illness Vicky had decided that if she was going to have cancer then she would make some positive use of it, and not just for herself. She would wring the benefits out of cancer and make them widely available. But how was she to achieve this? Her midnight cogitations in her diaries and many long conversations with her close friends revolved around this concern.

Her experience with the cancer groups made her appreciate what a potent source of information as well as support lay within them. But they were all small, local efforts and there were so few of them, certainly not anything like enough to meet the needs of the million people in this country who are estimated to be living with cancer at any given moment, or the 200,000 people who are newly diagnosed with it each year. She knew that the groups were little known about and very difficult to find. You might hear of their existence through a chance remark or because you had been exceptionally persistent.

You might even be the sort of person who felt impelled to set up such a group because of your own problems but your energies were unlikely to extend beyond the immediate circle. Just occasionally, you might be fortunate enough to find yourself in a hospital like Barts where the oncologist actually encouraged their existence. This last was a very rare circumstance because most doctors, as Vicky was soon to discover, were still deeply suspicious of anything that smacked of patient self-help or indeed any kind of lay organization that could possibly be seen to question their professional judgement or status.

In general, Vicky felt that health professionals were not guilty of the more crass prejudices that can so deeply wound cancer patients. Nonetheless, she was disturbed by the conspiracy of silence that she found surrounded cancer, as much within medical circles as without. Her numerous contacts and conversations with patients, as another patient, served only to strengthen her conviction that it was a great mistake to assume that people with cancer were 'happier' if they did not know too much about their disease. Patients were asking her all the time for more information and more detailed explanations of what they could expect from their treatment. She was not on her own in her need for information to help her cope better.

Cancer had been locked into a closet. Vicky was determined to kick it out once and for all.

Back in November 1983 when Vicky was still sunk in gloom and wondering what to do with her life she had written: 'Depression — is work a symptom of it or a cause of it? Why am I having such a violent reaction to work? Is it because it was so important to me before — the reason for living — and now having been ill and stopped for fourteen months, I have got life but lost my nerve for work and in some ways I feel dead. As work is so important to me because I have these agonies now, so [it is necessary] to substitute something for death of my love for research in medicine at Barts.'

In May 1984, even before she had gone into hospital, she had begun to have inklings of what that substitute might be. On 19th May Alison and Michael had come to supper and they had had a 'chat re British Cancer Support Society'. Also before that weekend illness, Vicky had met Dr Robert Buckman, a young Canadian doctor who had himself recently suffered from a life-threatening disease (not cancer) which had radically altered his ideas about the way doctors should treat their patients. Immediately after the hospital interlude she met a couple of other people who were professionally connected with voluntary organizations.

By Monday, 11th June, after a day spent thinking about her support society while working in the lab, she decided she should talk to Maurice Slevin about it. She fixed an appointment for the following day at six in the evening.

'I told Vicky that it sounded like a good idea but if it were that good why hadn't someone else come up with it? Or perhaps they had?'

Maurice gave her idea a cautious welcome. He knew, of course, all about Vicky's views on the importance of informing patients. It was a philosophy in which he too believed and they had discussed many times the things that patients had told her. He was impressed by the way she had participated in his cancer support group and he could see how this new idea fitted in very well with her belief that cancer should not be hidden away from public view. He agreed with her that the fear and misunderstanding enmeshing the disease, sometimes with tragic consequences, would not disappear until these attitudes changed.

Vicky asked Maurice that very same evening, 12th June 1984, to join her in setting up the organization. He quite frankly admits that he was not prepared to commit himself on the spot. He wanted to gain some idea as to the way medical colleagues he respected would react: both to the idea itself and to Vicky. He did, after all, have his own career to consider and he knew as well as anyone how conventional most of his fellow doctors were. If he were to be associated with something regarded as even slightly cranky or 'alternative' it could do him lasting damage. So he gave Vicky introductions to some of the top names in oncology and advised her to find out as much as she could about what was going on in the world of cancer beyond the hospital gates.

Six days later she was back in his office reporting progress and even Maurice, who by this time knew Vicky well, had to confess that he was 'amazed' by what she had achieved so far. She had had another talk with Robert Buckman, written to fifteen cancer organizations, made appointments with several of them and spoken to many more people about the idea. Returning home after her talk with Maurice, she and Tim discussed who should be president of the organization.

By the end of June, only three weeks after she had first broached the project with Maurice, she had met many of the people who were to give her enormous help in the next few months and years. Friday, 29th June, was her last full day at work in the laboratory. It marked the closing of a significant chapter in her life and the end of her once promising career in endocrinological research. Yet it passed almost without comment except that she and Tim had a celebratory dinner at Pollyanna's Bistro in Battersea. More important, obviously, was the fact that on that same day she had established contact with Bryan Skinner, a prominent businessman living in Jersey. He was a patient of Dr Peter Wrigley, an oncologist colleague of Maurice Slevin, and she had telephoned him that afternoon as soon as she had his number. 'He sounds great,' she comments in her diary. The following day she woke at six in the morning 'mind all abuzz – so exciting'. She went back to Barts to clear up all her outstanding clinic letters and finish off some assays and that was it. She was not due to start her GP training until September so she was now free to devote the rest of the summer to her cancer society.

Vicky was starting from scratch and what she knew about setting up and running an organization could have been written on the back of a postage stamp. Why indeed should she know anything? She had never been interested in party politics or any other kind of pressure group activity or campaigning which required organizational and committee skills. Until now her life had been set on quite another track and all her energies had been concentrated on achieving the task in hand as well as possible, both for its own sake and for her own satisfaction. Vicky never allowed herself to lapse from her own high ideals, established while she was still at school, of doing everything on which she had set her heart and her hand as perfectly as possible. If this organization was to become a reality then she intended it to be first class in every way. That meant it had to be thoroughly professional. Vicky had no time for amateurs, no matter how gifted.

She turned to Tim for advice on political and organizational strategies and her introductions to business men like Bryan Skinner and Michael Silverman, another cancer survivor, were also to prove very important. They introduced her to the mysteries of finance. She learnt about business plans and sources for funding. They talked about offices, staff recruitment, management, the similarities and the differences between running a charitable trust and a business. It began to dawn on Vicky that she had set upon a very complicated project and that she had a huge amount to learn. The prospect of the challenge only whetted her appetite for more.

In July the pace hotted up. Maurice had given her some more medical names to contact. Each introduction led to several more and, since she never missed a single opportunity to meet anyone who might have something to offer her, she had soon encountered many more people than either she or Maurice could ever have envisaged. She may not, at this early stage, have had much under her belt in the way of financial or organizational skills but in one respect Vicky was always very well endowed. Her enthusiasm for anything that she believed in was enormously infectious and she backed it up with remarkable powers of persuasion. She had no problem in exploiting this talent now. Few people could resist her appeal to join her. And there was one aspect of her previous life which certainly came in useful at this early stage. Her experience of giving papers to eminent and learned audiences made her less abashed than she might otherwise have been about seeking out any distinguished people she thought could help in other fields.

The late Professor Tim McElwain was one of these. As a well-respected senior medical oncologist at the Royal Marsden Hospital in Sutton, Maurice was particularly keen that she should make contact with him. Vicky typed a letter to the professor on 5th July and made a note to herself that if she had not heard in a week, she would ring him, which she duly did, but still no joy. What followed was a story that Tim McElwain always enjoyed telling. A fortnight had passed and still Vicky had not received a reply. She discovered that he lived quite near to her in Clapham so, over the following weekend, she drove round to his house planning to call on him and arrange an appointment there and then. As it happened, he was working in his front garden.

'Are you Professor Tim McElwain?' she asked him.

'Yes.'

'The man I want,' said Vicky with a big smile, whereupon with what seemed like a hop and a skip she walked up his garden path and proceeded without further ado to explain who she was and why she had decided she could not wait any longer for his reply.

'It was the best proposal I'd had in years,' Tim used to chuckle. Like most people, he was immediately disarmed by Vicky's enthusiasm and sure knowledge of what she wanted. They made an appointment to meet in his office the following week and, on Thursday, 19th July, Vicky drove to Sutton, feeling very nervous but 'what a great meeting' it turned out to be. They talked for two and a half hours and found they agreed on many things. He said he hated quackery but Vicky assured him that there would be nothing like that in her organization. They had a sandwich lunch together and she felt a great load off her mind now that such a big shot in cancer medicine was supporting her. Mac, as he was known to his friends and colleagues, was a big man in every way. He would, in the years to come, become a close friend of Vicky and Tim, as well as exert a powerful influence on the fledgling organization.

Vicky drove back to Barts where she had an appointment with the Dean. He gave his permission for her to use the Guild Room for the meeting that she was planning and he too pledged his support to her British Association of Cancer Patients and their Families. What a good day it had been!

She had first formulated a name for her cancer society in a document dated 10th July which she was sending out to doctors, patients and other people who she had been told might have a positive contribution to make. It is a model of clarity and shows how even at this early stage – only a month after she had had her first long talk with Maurice Slevin – Vicky knew exactly what kind of organization she wanted to found. Later she would produce a more polished and refined version but her essential priorities never changed.

It was to be a national umbrella organization for all patients with malignant disease. She stated that although there were already in existence two major cancer relief organizations and several smaller societies for people suffering from a particular cancer, there remained an unfilled gap for patients with malignant disease which she believed would be 'better served' by her prospective organization. Vicky had done her homework. But of course! She had visited them all so was now able to list every significant cancer organization in the country and encapsulate its main function. She then briefly described the purpose of her association as she saw it:

> to offer practical help, advice and information to patients and relatives. It would have charitable status; be located in central London and run by professionals, both medical and non-medical.

Vicky elaborated on what she intended by 'practical help' in her following paragraph which I quote here in full because it is interesting to see how closely Vicky followed her own original brief when the time came to establish BACUP.

> Part of the charity's initial remit would be to provide through its medical specialist advisers, patient information leaflets about cancer in general, aspects of treatment, where to turn for specific practical help and site-specific information about malignant disease; the Association will provide a telephone advice service and letter reply service as well as produce a newsletter or journal of the Association which will keep patients and relatives informed of the activities of the Association and its members as well as provide information on progress in basic research, early detection of cancer, treatment and diagnostic techniques. We would aim eventually to establish a national network of suitably carefully selected, trained and supervised ex-patients and relatives who could provide practical advice and support to individual patients. The

establishment of a national network of voluntary helpers who would also help to provide for the day-to-day needs of cancer patients and their families.

Everything in that mission statement is present in BACUP today, except for the establishment of a patient volunteer network. That is under active consideration now and may well form part of the expanding BACUP counselling service.

Vicky concluded her document with two important statements. The first was her very firm commitment to conventional medicine. She believed it was important to publicize the positive benefits of orthodox treatment – the proliferation of 'alternative' cancer treatments was just beginning to take off, a development which was underpinned by the growing fame of the Bristol Cancer Help Centre. Although Vicky herself had earlier expressed an interest in relaxation, transcendental meditation and hypnotherapy – she had even booked herself on a course in hypnosis in October – she was now veering away from these 'fringe' areas because she realized that if she was to achieve the powerful medical support she wanted for her organization she would have to stress its orthodox, non-controversial nature.

This was not a difficult decision for Vicky to make. Her scientific mind and her strong bias to seek always the rational solution made her naturally distrustful of any treatment that smacked of mysticism or quackery, or 'cures' based on wishful thinking rather than rigorous testing. Later she would become more entrenched in this viewpoint, yet there had always been a part of Vicky which was intellectually intrigued by the subtle, inexplicable influences the mind can have on the body. She it was, after all, who had written the original paper which appeared in *Nature*, showing that there was indeed a link between the endogenous opiates (pain killers) occurring naturally in the brain and the use of acupuncture to control pain. (The Chinese have been using acupuncture for this purpose, among others, for something like 3,000 years.)

It would be fair to say that Vicky's interest in the non-physical aspects of medicine became submerged rather than totally banished. She felt there were undoubtedly complementary therapies which did work but her scientific mind wanted them to be submitted to the rigours of clinical trials. By the time BACUP had become a formal concept she no longer had time for anything but making this particular dream come true. She would have to leave it to others to explore the side alleys of the psyche. All the same when, a year later, she spoke to Anthony Clare about BACUP in her radio interview, she stressed her belief that conventional medicine could and should be as holistic in its approach as the complementary therapies. She did not believe that there was anything about the treatments *per se* which precluded doctors and nurses from ministering to the psychological and spiritual needs of their patients as well as the purely physical aspects of care.

Her second, and to her mind, 'equally important' point was that there was an absolute need for

one recognized national body where cancer patients and their relatives feel they can belong and contribute to, and, in this way, help others and themselves during the disease.

Not only was she convinced of the need; she now knew for an absolute certainty that she had conceived that organization.

It officially became BACUP — British Association of Cancer United Patients and their families and friends — in July 1984. The acronym BACUP was Maurice Slevin's idea: 'I very rarely have such inspiration but it felt right immediately.' He intended a silent 'U' but it was Tim who pointed out that it could be used to mean 'United', thereby conveying the all-important concept that patients are united with each other as well as their families and friends. Vicky hoped it did not sound too much like a football team. By this time Maurice was whole-heartedly committed to BACUP and was giving Vicky all the support he could.

On Wednesday, 18th July a teacher gave Vicky her first donation for BACUP in pennies and halfpennies. Now she knew for certain that BACUP existed.

Her pace of life had augmented rather than decreased. Apart from tiring easily which she tried to counter by taking frequent cat naps, she felt extremely well and bouncy. All the same a bout of diarrhoea and a temperature had made her visit Maurice for a check-up. They both felt that she had probably been overdoing it, as usual, but that the holiday would put her right.

The last week of July in the run-up to her departure to the States was frantic. She had a number of letters to write in relation to BACUP as well as some work to complete before leaving from Heathrow on Saturday. At the same time she was collecting as many introductions and addresses of cancer organizations as possible because she intended this to be a working holiday. Somehow in the middle of all this frenetic activity she managed to find time to spend two days at Cambridge, attending an endocrinological meeting with Sue Jackson, a colleague from Barts. She made some contributions to the meeting and enjoyed renewing her acquaintance with other researchers whom she had known quite well in past times. It was a subdued swansong for a memorable career.

The American holiday was a tremendous success. She and Tim stayed with friends, first in Canada and then they travelled on through the States stopping first with David and Marietta Esterley. This was the occasion, mentioned previously, when

Vicky learned to play baseball. On 2nd August she noted in her diary with an obvious note of triumph that she played tennis for the first time since August 1982. It was her 'first strenuous physical activity since ill' and she won a doubles match with David as her partner. From the Esterleys they went to Maine and stayed with Vicky's brother George and his wife and then on to Boston, Washington (where they stayed with Robert, Tim's younger brother, and his wife Linda) and New York, staying with other friends.

She was, however, working at the same time. After giving herself a week's complete break she was on the telephone fixing appointments to visit all the major cancer organizations and anyone else who could give her help. Her visits included the National Cancer Institute in Washington and the Cancer Information Service in Baltimore, Boston and New York. Also in New York she visited the American Cancer Society, the Sloan Kettering Memorial Cancer Hospital and the charity Cancer Care. She was fascinated by what the Americans were doing. She could see that they were far ahead of Britain insofar as providing an information service was concerned but she was well aware that the more closed, introvert British personality might not be attracted by the American style. This did not, however, diminish her enthusiasm for her own project. It would be a challenge to find a way of adapting what the Americans were already doing so successfully. Eventually she would improve on it. She returned to England laden down with two suitcases crammed full of pamphlets, leaflets, videos and other material.

By 31st August 1984, Vicky had contacted twenty-four cancer organizations in the United Kingdom, seven in America and one each in Dublin, Switzerland and Zimbabwe. This is quite apart from the scores of people to whom she had talked. She had learnt so much, she could hardly believe it herself but nothing had shaken her conviction that there was no organization quite like BACUP yet in existence. There *was* a need for it and she was the person to bring it into being.

Strengthening her view in this respect were three people she had met in these months, all of whom had made a great impression on her. In order of their appearance in Vicky's second life, first was Elizabeth Ward, the dynamic founder and director of the British Kidney Patient Association, who has fought passionately for a better deal for all kidney patients ever since her own son was diagnosed with renal failure in 1966 at the age of thirteen. Vicky had visited Mrs Ward at her home in Hampshire and was hugely impressed by the way she ran the whole operation from her desk in a crowded study: dictating letters, answering the telephone herself, signing all the cheques and doing most of the fund-raising.

'I thought if this lady can do it,' Vicky later told me, 'we're going to do it for cancer patients.'

Next was Bryan Skinner, the Chairman of a large company and a successful businessman who had been stricken by cancer. He became Vicky's guide, mentor and friend and was to give her invaluable help with setting up BACUP.

'If you do not have a dream, it will never come true,' he told Vicky, words which she would treasure.

Finally, shortly after she returned from America, she paid a visit to Andrew Phillips, a solicitor friend of Tim's, for advice on how to make BACUP a charity. He had never met Vicky before but within five minutes of hearing her tell her story and explain her reasons for wanting to set up BACUP, he realized that here was someone with a great clarity of purpose and sense of priority who was also quite astonishingly bright.

'I recognized that she was one of these unusual animals who is highly motivated, clear-minded, decisive and absolutely able to do what she wanted to achieve. She had suffered through to her own personal conclusion and what she now had was a vision.'

Vicky convinced him that there was nothing aery-fairy about this vision; it was down to earth and practical as she was herself. Once he had satisfied himself that she really had thoroughly explored the whole cancer scene and that she was determined to pursue her own path rather than work through some other organization already in existence, he looked at this 'little woman sparking away with many more volts than the size of her battery indicated', and took a deep breath. He told her that if she was serious about getting this charity up and running there could be no half measures. She could not expect to run it part-time, something to do on the side with someone else at the helm, while she continued her career. She would have to take full control: become the chairman and chief executive and work at it full time.

Vicky was taken aback by his suggestion. She was about to start training as a GP. How could she possible throw all that overboard, having set her heart on her change of career and having prepared the ground so carefully? Besides, was it not a rather preposterous notion? She had no executive experience. But Andrew Phillips was insistent. 'I was forceful with her and I told her it won't work unless *you* make it work. Everything about her and her situation made me convinced that this woman had to do her thing like no one else I'd ever met.'

He admits that immediately after Vicky walked out of his office, saying she would have to think over what he had said, he did feel some concern. Had he been too emphatic? After all, he knew very little about her and her circumstances but he had been possessed by a hunch he could not ignore. From past experience he knew that it was sometimes vital to let his intuition drive his intellect, as it had done on this occasion.

Vicky's friends were not nearly so sure that BACUP was something Vicky should be doing, or even that it was a particularly good idea. All through the summer she had been discussing her dream with David and Alison and Michael and they had been giving her a rather negative feedback. It upset her when she had time to think about it but she did understand their reservations. Here was their dear friend whom they had tenderly cared for during the long months of illness and recuperation. Now that she was well again they naturally wanted to enjoy her company, have fun with the old laughing 'Vicks' and forget about the illness. Could she not put her cancer behind her? Why must she start on something so ambitious? She would overdo things again, thus running the risk of becoming ill once more. Was this organization needed anyway?

Tim never had a moment of doubt that it was necessary to support Vicky in this new venture. From the day she had first tentatively discussed it with him, some four months earlier, he had been wholeheartedly supportive. He believed her when she said: 'I *really believe* in it – probably more than anything I have ever done before.' He realized the risks Vicky was running but he also understood, as perhaps no one else did, her need to find a cause and fight for it. He was never to waver in that conviction.

David was the next to succumb to Vicky's persuasive powers. Initially, he was not all that keen on the idea itself but the more Vicky talked about it the more he began to understand what she was trying to do. He did worry about Vicky's health. This project had grown out of all recognition compared with the ideas she had discussed with him earlier. However, when he realized that Vicky was not to be shaken off and that she did seem to have grasped the magnitude of the undertaking, he felt he could not do other than give her his full support.

Shortly after the American holiday Vicky and Tim went round to supper to visit Alison and Michael for the first time in their new home. BACUP came up for discussion and Vicky expounded all her ideas: the telephone information service, the newspaper for patients, leaflets, a national network, possibly a club. The friends misjudged the situation. As was their wont, they treated the subject as if it were no more than another debating point. Everyone present, apart from Tim, was a doctor so they began along the lines of 'Do we really need this kind of organization? Isn't it a very middle-class idea to think patients want information? Who would run it?'

Over the years they had had so many of these loud, argumentative evenings that it dawned too late on Alison and Michael and Mark, another old friend also present, that this time was different. The goalposts had been moved. Vicky was not prepared to discuss BACUP in a detached manner, as merely an idea that she was airing with them in order to seek their opinions. BACUP was already conceived. She was passionately committed to it and the time had long since passed for criticizing it in any form, intellectually or on practical grounds. In fact, as they realized later, whatever misgivings they might harbour about BACUP itself, as far as the nitty-gritty of setting up a charity was concerned they would have had little to offer then in the way of constructive criticism since they had grossly underestimated just how much groundwork Vicky had already put into the project. Possibly they should have known better, since they knew from old that Vicky was obsessively thorough in anything she took on. And she had, after all, been talking to them all summer about her plans.

The evening ended dismally with angry words and everyone feeling very unhappy. Her friends knew then that Vicky was set on a course from which she would not be diverted. They loved her and they wanted the best for her but already they could sense that BACUP was taking her away from them. They were losing her to all those people out there who were said to be struggling in confusion and isolation and in desperate need of help. Vicky was rejecting her closest friends for all those unnamed, unknown strangers in the future.

The wounds were later healed but the pain they had caused

could never be quite forgotten. A few days later Vicky was staying with her sister Tina in Switzerland from where she wrote a long letter to Alison and Michael. Once again she explained her reasons for going ahead with BACUP and why she felt that she must run it. She recognized that she was asking a lot of herself and her friends but begged them to support her in this arduous journey she had resolved to make. She wanted them to accompany her on it; she needed them, especially when the going got tough as she knew it would, but also she hoped they would share her joys. She described how she was already being called on to help patients, mainly with information and encouragement. 'It doesn't take very much to help people – we just need to organize it.' She had been convinced by Andrew Phillips's insistence that she must lead this organization if she wanted it to succeed but she had been wounded by their suggestion that she was giving everything else up, including them, to embark on an ego trip. She admitted that there were benefits in it for her, but what was so wrong about that? She did not, after all, have children and she knew better than anyone that her life was under threat. Could she not, therefore, choose to do what she wanted with what remained to her of it? The cancer might come back at any time. All she hoped for was that she would stay well long enough to establish BACUP on a firm footing.

'Life is about choices . . . I like talking to people about these ideas and the rewards in terms of how you can help cancer patients and their families are incredible . . . thus I am doing something for myself and fulfilling the need to help others.'

It is an eloquent and moving letter, Vicky's apologia, and it ends on an impassioned note. 'I know it is a dream, and a rather grand dream at that – but I am convinced it is possible and will leave no stone unturned in the search of advice, funds etc. to make it a reality.'

12

A Shifting Horizon

❖

T HE FIRST BACUP Working Party meeting was held in
the Guild Room at St Bartholomew's Hospital, on 31st
October 1984. About forty people had been invited;
twenty-nine attended. There were representatives from the
major cancer organizations, senior cancer doctors, big names
from the City and others whom Vicky had checked out carefully and had invited because she felt they would make a
useful contribution. Among those who sent their apologies
were Dame Mary Donaldson, then Lord Mayor of London,
and the late Stuart Young, then Chairman of the BBC Board
of Governors. Both were later to prove great friends and
supporters of BACUP.

Anyone who was present on that occasion will surely never
forget it. There was a barely suppressed shiver of excited
anticipation running round the room, an unmistakable sense of
being in at the start of something important; yet we were largely
strangers to each other, most of us able to pick out a recognizable
face only here and there from our own field. I was there as a
medical journalist who had written a book on breast cancer.
Vicky, however, already knew us all quite well, having spent
many hours discussing her ideas about BACUP with each one
of us. Now here she was, this slight young woman, the self-
styled Convenor of First Meeting, sitting at the head of a
large oval table around which the rest of us were crowded in
rows two deep.

No one watching her perform that evening would have believed that it was the first time in her life that she had chaired such an event; indeed, that it was the first time she had even attended a meeting of this ilk. As a busy research worker with no taste for politics — medical or any other — Vicky had had no occasion in her previous life to sit on a committee of any kind. Yet here she was, running this meeting like a veteran: self-possessed and completely in control. She took us through the ten-point agenda smoothly and adroitly: introductions were effected; the general objectives of BACUP were agreed and then, item by item, the crucial plans for the new organization were discussed. Vicky had already prioritized them before the meeting into 'immediate' and 'future'.

Immediate plans agreed that evening were to:

1 Establish a comprehensive Cancer Information Service by telephone and mail
2 Provide a comprehensive range of educational information leaflets
3 Produce a quarterly newspaper to communicate regularly with cancer patients and their families and friends
4 Cooperate with other cancer organizations with similar interests in relation to patients but without sacrificing BACUP's uniqueness.

'Immediate' meant exactly that for Vicky, so it is not surprising, although nonetheless remarkable, to note that everything tabled under that heading rolled right into action from the day BACUP started functioning.

Vicky's 'future' plans are in the process of being implemented, but it is reasonable to guess that, had she lived long enough, they would by now have already become reality.

They were to:

1 Set up a network of regional contact points for support, fund-raising and educational purposes
2 Investigate the setting up of a 'patient to patient'
volunteer programme where trained and supervised
veteran patients could counsel and help other
patients
3 Set up a 'Helping Hand' network based on the regional contact points where voluntary helpers could
provide for some of the day to day needs of cancer
patients.

Next came the all-important question of structure. Vicky
had taken careful advice from her lawyer, Andrew Phillips,
Tim, and her business friends, Bryan Skinner in particular. She
had also spent some time visiting other charities, not just
those in the cancer field, to discover how they were organized
and what she might expect could go wrong. She did not want
to waste any time on re-inventing the wheel or undoing
expensive mistakes. BACUP had to be right from the work go.
And the 'off' was going to be that night, a fact that few of the
participants, other than Vicky and her closest advisers, would
have realized when they received their invitations. She announced that the charity had already been set up: three trustees
had been appointed — herself, Maurice Slevin and Professor
Kenneth Calman — and now it was necessary to appoint a
steering committee willing to take the project forward until, in
six months' time, it became a company limited by guarantee.
The steering committee would then convert into an executive
committee and continue functioning, much as a board of direc-
tors operates within a company.

The appointment of officers and members of the steering
committee was an entirely 'non-random process' as Maurice
Slevin has since cheerfully admitted, and everyone eventually

realized, many of them some time after the event. At the time the Working Party might have thought it was voting freely for the steering committee; well, it did vote, but in fact it was voting for Vicky's nominees. As she said to me much later, it was a matter of 'nobbling various people beforehand', telling them what she wanted them to do, and then asking others to act as their nominators and seconders.

It all went through almost on the nod: Vicky was voted Chairman and Chief Executive; Maurice Slevin became deputy Chairman; Professor Tim McElwain was Chairman of the Medical and Specialist Advisory Board; and Dr Peter Wrigley, in his absence, was elected Chairman of the Fund Raising/Resources Committee. Three more doctors were voted on to the steering committee – Professors Kenneth Calman and Anthony Clare, and Dr Peter McGuire – but there was only one other cancer patient – Dame Mary Donaldson – apart from Vicky. These were heavyweight names and Vicky had done brilliantly in persuading them to throw their hats into her ring. She needed their calibre if she was to achieve the almost instant credibility with her profession that she saw as essential to the success of BACUP.

There is no doubt that she was correct in making that assumption but the strong medical presence which has always existed in the organization has also made it vulnerable to the charge that it is over-influenced by medical perspectives. It is, after all, an organization for cancer patients which has, as its stated aims:

> relief by any and every charitable means of the poverty, distress and/or ignorance of those who have, had or are suspected of having cancer and of their families and friends.

The very reason why Vicky felt BACUP was necessary in the first place could also be seen as a reason why doctors should not be allowed too much of a hand in its development. Many of the clients who would use BACUP in the future would be doing so precisely because they had not received enough information or support from their doctors and other health carers.

Vicky had no problem refuting this criticism. She believed firmly in professionalism and, in her book, that meant never settling for anything less than the best. She had sounded out each of these doctors very carefully, just as she had sounded out everyone else in that room. She knew she could be certain of their commitment to her idea because anyone with half a doubt would not have staked their medical future on alliance to such a bold and risky venture. One senior professor of surgery to whom Vicky outlined her plans afterwards telephoned the mutual friend who had effected the introduction and, without preamble, in tones half admiring, half concerned, said: 'You've sent me dynamite.'

Several other doctors Vicky had approached earlier did express misgivings; some had been frankly hostile. The dubious ones would have worried that patients would be alarmed by all this 'unnecessary' information and what good would it do them anyway? Those who were more strongly opposed – and there are some who still are today – would take the view that their patients should listen only to them, take what is offered without discussion and that if they 'dare' to seek further information or a second opinion they are thereby threatening their doctor's authority or questioning his (or her) competence. Vicky wasted no time trying to persuade them to change their views at that stage. Let BACUP prove its worth in due course and meanwhile she was more than happy with the medical support she had won.

The meeting proceeded to a satisfactory conclusion. Priorities for immediate action had been established. These centred mainly around setting up the Cancer Information Service and each task would have been enough to keep one full-time researcher occupied for half a year. Vicky undertook to get them all underway and to report back on progress at the next Steering Committee meeting, fixed for five weeks hence. At that point she had received private donations amounting to £39,000, a major one coming from her father, but BACUP had neither staff nor premises. The appointment of a Project Co-ordinator whose salary could be guaranteed for two years was agreed to be a matter of urgency. Everyone else would be giving their services and time voluntarily but they would be relying on Vicky to tell them what she wanted from them.

It was noted in the minutes that the aim was to launch BACUP in not more than a year from that evening. Heads turned towards the Chinese firecracker sitting at the head of the table. Would she be able to deliver?

Only Vicky's closest friends and associates knew what a truly loaded, unspoken question that was. She had had a recurrence of cancer.

Vicky was always quite open about describing the state of her health so everyone present would probably have been aware of that fact. However, most of us that evening would not have appreciated what the implications of that diagnosis would be for her subsequent treatment. I, for example, had met Vicky in Oxford in late September at a conference organized by the British Holistic Medical Association. Although we had met only once before, she immediately told me that she had been diagnosed with a recurrence. She did not exactly laugh it off but she did suggest that it was a nuisance rather than a trauma which would merely involve a short stay in hospital.

The reality of the situation was that just ten days before this inaugural BACUP meeting took place she had left hospital after another major operation. The tumour had grown again and spread to other organs. As she explained in a letter to an

American friend: 'some three hours into the operation the surgeon found it technically impossible not to remove the rectum as well as part of the sigmoid colon'. She was left with a permanent colostomy. This means a bag is attached to an opening in the abdominal wall to collect all the faecal matter normally passed through the rectum. The patient has to learn how to live with this disability and cope with changing the bag.

She and Tim were shocked and devastated. No one, including Maurice and her other doctors, had thought this would happen. Unlike her hysterectomy in 1982 when she had been prepared for the possibility by talking to a stoma nurse who is specially trained to advise and help patients living with this type of stomach-related problem, this time there had been no pre-operative counselling. There followed what she recalled in this same letter quoted above as 'a stormy post-operative period'. Not only did she have to try to come to terms with what had happened but she had to cope with serious complications and pain so severe that finally she was given a subcutaneous infusion of a morphine compound. The worst problem of all she found was having to accept that the colostomy was permanent. Its presence on her body and all the new routines she now had to learn to handle served as a constant reminder of her cancer.

Her anger and her grief subsided faster than did Tim's who felt appalled and helpless on her behalf. But they comforted each other and, in her typical fashion, Vicky quickly pulled herself together and set about learning practical tips for coping with her new situation. 'It's like travelling with a baby, really,' she told me. 'You have to be so vigilant and so careful and plan for everything but you just carry a bigger handbag to cart all the gear around, and you manage. I learned, just as thousands of others people have had to learn.'

*

When Vicky first knew that her cancer had come back she considered very seriously whether she should go ahead with her BACUP project. She feared that all the enthusiasm she had generated and offers of support that had come pouring in might melt away if it got out that she were ill once more. On the other hand, she could see no point in concealing her condition. The truth would be revealed in the end anyway.

Her relapse happened at a very bad time. Tim was very occupied with the Liberal Conference. Her friend David was on holiday in Greece. She had to cancel several BACUP related appointments including a trip to Holland to visit a cancer information service. After a week of tests, the biopsy result came through on the Friday, confirming beyond doubt that she had cancer again. Vicky was very depressed.

And then something extraordinary happened which transformed her despair into hope. Earlier in September she had received a letter from an American cancer survivor, Jay Weinberg, who had started an imaginative scheme called Corporate Angel Network which links up cancer patients who need to travel with the near empty, company-owned aircraft flying their executives between cities. He had been given Vicky's name as someone to contact in London and so he had written, suggesting they meet. He and his wife flew into London that same weekend after Vicky had received the bad news.

The Weinbergs were staying in Grosvenor House and invited Vicky to breakfast on Sunday morning. Over the coffee and croissants it all came spilling out: her plans for BACUP; what she had done so far; and now this dilemma. What should she do? Mr Weinberg then told her that he had had not one but two primary cancers – a melanoma thirty years ago and, more recently, cancer of the colon. He had also been through a recurrence. All this while continuing his career and being – as Vicky intended to be though this was not yet clear to her – a well-known public figure. When the second cancer had occurred he was in the midst of fronting a major fund-raising programme for the renowned Sloan Kettering cancer hospital in New York. He had been in the same quandary as Vicky now found herself but, after discussing the matter from every angle with his friends and fellow campaigners, they had come to the conclusion that honesty was the best policy. Jay Weinberg had his operation, recovered from it and continued to lead the campaign which benefited rather than suffered from his openness. He urged Vicky to follow his example – to be herself and to be honest about her cancer.

She felt greatly heartened by his story. Here was a man who had been through what she was now going through and had survived, triumphantly. It inspired her and turned her round. From that moment Vicky knew that she had something more to work for than just her health. She had BACUP to create and nurture and lead.

Just before this encounter Vicky met someone else who was to play a key role in the formation of BACUP. Her name was Yvonne Terry and she was then studying for an MSc in Sociology applied to Medicine. She had done her nursing training at Barts twenty years earlier and, after a good nursing career in the hospital, ending up as a senior sister in the medical oncology unit, she had temporarily broken off to pursue full-time academic study. When she met Vicky she was doing a research study with leukaemia patients to discover their particular needs but was finding it frustrating because the patients were really too ill to want to talk to her. Meanwhile the doctors were trying to use her as a counsellor which she felt was inappropriate.

Maurice Slevin introduced the two women when Vicky was in the Pitcairn ward for her tests. Like everyone who came into Vicky's orbit, Yvonne was enthused by her enthusiasm. She also recognized the patients' needs that Vicky had identified and agreed with her that they were not being met by the health professionals. Her experience as a cancer nurse had taught her how much unhappiness can arise within families where there is cancer, often stemming from lies uttered to 'protect' the patient from the truth or a relative from facing up to the inevitable. Just as hurtful is the rejection that many patients feel their illness has brought upon them. Yvonne had her own personal reason for being interested in BACUP. Both her parents had had cancer and she had suffered deeply from the experience: one parent had denied it and the other had become very angry and difficult to live with.

Vicky asked Yvonne if she would consider running the BACUP Information Service and Yvonne said yes, in principle. She had to wait, of course, until after the Working Party meeting to know whether the organization was even going to get off the ground. The post of Project Co-ordinator which was to be her title would have to be approved and, finally, she would have to go through the standard appointment procedures. As if these were not hurdles enough, there was also Vicky's operation to surmount but, despite the uncertainties, Yvonne was prepared to give it a go. She was inspired, like so many others, by Vicky's determination and courage.

Just as soon as Vicky was feeling better after her major surgery and had recovered her mental equilibrium, she was hard at work dictating letters for her temporary typist at home and ringing people from her hospital bed, using a portable telephone that Tim had bought for her. Andrew Phillips pulled out all the violin stops with the Charity Commissioners, not hesitating to emphasize Vicky's plight, and succeeded in making BACUP a charitable trust within forty-eight hours, probably a record. The papers were all signed by Vicky in her hospital bed. Elizabeth Sturgeon, a friend and former editor with Heinemann, had agreed to work voluntarily as the secretary to BACUP and she helped Vicky prepare the agenda. Yvonne did all she could at the hospital end, including stuffing the envelopes. Assisted by her friends and supporters, Vicky achieved a quite remarkable feat: she arrived on the last day of that momentous, at times awful, month to conduct the first meeting of her life with all the panache and skill of a seasoned committee woman.

She had two other successes that month which she described with some satisfaction in a letter to an American friend, Linda Powers. The first was to persuade Stuart Young, that her as yet unborn organization was important and needed television coverage and support for fund-raising. She had her meeting with him on 2nd October, the morning she was admitted to hospital. The second, even more remarkable feat, was to keep her promise to give a talk, 'Cancer – the Patient's View' to the College of Health.

Many months earlier, Marianne Rigge, the Director, had invited Vicky to be the guest speaker at the College's first annual conference on 6th October, to address an audience of 300 people. Vicky particularly wanted to give this talk. She had prepared the text and it would be her first opportunity to speak to a wide, largely lay audience about her experiences as a cancer patient and what she dreamed about doing to improve the lot of all cancer patients. However, as the time drew nearer and the date was fixed for her operation – 4th October – she knew she had no chance of recovering in time to keep her appointment. Suddenly, she had a brainwave. Why not make a video and ask the College to run it in lieu of her presence?

No sooner thought than done. She persuaded the audio-visual department at Barts to make a video and she spoke her text to camera – unrehearsed – like an old pro. It was received very well by the College of Health's audience and later became a useful publicity tool for BACUP.

Although Vicky had come to terms with the knowledge that her cancer had returned, it had been a sad, bitter time for her, as she freely acknowledged to Linda Powers, in that same long letter she wrote her, dated 21st November 1984. This was after Vicky had had further special but extremely painful and difficult treatment, this time in another London hospital, the only place where it was then available. She had decided to submit herself to the so-called 'magic bullet'. This was the radioactive monoclonal antibody treatment which was then still at the experimental stage. It involved a catheter being inserted into the abdomen through which a radioactive fluid is passed to knock out any remaining cancer cells. She was one of only twelve patients with primary ovarian cancer to be receiving this treatment and, probably, was the only one with microscopic (undetectable) disease.

As usual, she seemed to 'lurch from complication to complication'. Because of all her previous operations and the resulting adhesions her catheter had to be inserted through her old appendix scar and the reopened wound started to bleed. The radioactive fluid was only one fifth of the dose normally given but it still did not distribute well throughout her abdomen. Her problems were intensified by finding herself in a ward where she described the conditions as 'medieval' and the nursing offhand, verging on the cruel.

She wrote to Linda in uncharacteristic detail about her medical problems because Linda was a cancer patient too, suffering from a brain tumour. Vicky did not know her well. She had met her through her brother George but she was able to relate with Linda in the direct spontaneous way that she was able to communicate with so many other cancer patients. She talked about the pain and grief she had suffered as well as the physical problems − 'I did my share of crying and not being brave' − and then described her way of bringing order out of the chaos that had threatened to engulf her.

'These were very hard times − one minute about to start a new career and planning the next five, ten or fifteen years −

and the next the uncertainty of the future, not just whether one would survive or not but that one would have to go through the treatment process possibly all over again ... my sights for the future have now been altered that I work on a six month to one year plan rather than thinking about things that I will do in two to three years ... I think of positive things which will come out of my current illness.'

One of those positive things was that she had to give up the idea of training to be a GP. Ever since Andrew Phillips had told her she must be in charge of BACUP full time if she intended it to succeed, she had been feeling overwhelmed by all that faced her. How was she to combine the two strands in her life, each of them full-time jobs? Now the decision had been taken out of her hands and she felt a keen sense of relief. She would be able to focus on BACUP alone and that was the major positive benefit resulting from her recurrence. BACUP was an 'activity programme', a project to which she felt totally committed and on which she would lavish all her energy and time.

The return of cancer had drawn her up sharply. She was back to an uncertain world. A hazardous journey with 'a shifting horizon' lay ahead of her, as she was later to tell Anthony Clare. But she was not going to spend too much time thinking about that. BACUP needed her and she needed BACUP. She was going to make her dream come true.

13

Window of Hope

❖

VICKY ALWAYS DID did her utmost to find a positive side to everything that befell her but this past hospital sojourn had sapped even her usually abundant optimism. Nonetheless, she did manage, from her hospital bed, to enter an application for a competition being run by *The Guardian* for charities. The prize was a computer which Vicky wanted for her new BACUP administration. Tim meanwhile was making himself 'a very useful courier' bringing her mail and messages, and she was even able to set up a few meetings and appointments for the end of November when she thought she would be strong enough to start about the business of BACUP again.

By the time she returned home, the family support system was already in place. Her mother had come back from Australia and her sister Betty was supplementing with cooked lunches and any other task she could fit in between looking after her two young sons. When Vicky first knew that the cancer had recurred, she had for a while quite seriously debated whether she would tell her family, not because she wanted to hide anything from them. Her concern was about a different matter. Although she appreciated everything her mother, in particular, had done for her, she had at times also felt rather 'taken over' and, if there was one thing Vicky hated more almost than anything, it was to lose control of any part of her life. She did not, therefore, now relish the prospect of having once again to rely on her family for help in running the house.

Many of Vicky's friends had marvelled at Susie's kind heart and endless willingness to do all that her daughter wanted. One summed it up for them all: 'She was a great provider – a warm maternal symbol.' But often Vicky couched her needs in somewhat imperative tones. She had an unconsciously literal way of describing her own actions, saying 'I sent so-and-so . . .' rather than 'I asked . . .' Later, when BACUP was established, she would often express the view that it helped relatives to cope with the illness of their loved one if the patient gave them tasks to perform. It made them feel useful. Well, certainly. But Vicky often made a request sound more like an order.

Another thing that worried Vicky was that her mother, in her understandable concern about her daughter's health, would try to stop her from doing things which Vicky would regard as essential, whereas Susie might fear that she was overdoing it again. Vicky eventually solved the problem by asking other members of the family to put pressure on her mother 'and convince her that if she were to come she must look after her own health and not mollycoddle me'. This desire not to be thwarted became more urgent as a BACUP began to take shape because, as she wrote in her long letter of 21st November to Linda Powers: 'particularly with my new organization to think of, I have something more to work for than just my health'.

By most people's standards Vicky was still pretty sick when she came out of hospital. She was feeling exhausted from the treatment which the doctors already suspected had not been successful, and her wound needed daily dressing. In a diary entry dated 20th November she described herself as 'not standing straight and tired' but she managed to go out to dinner with David and was thrilled to be in a restaurant again for the first time since her recurrence had been diagnosed. On 22nd November she went early to bed with a book and noted: 'first time not think of charity in ages – great'. It was to be one of very few respites she ever gave herself. The next day her mother-in-law came round with some food and Vicky expatiated on her plans for BACUP. The day after she was starting to think very hard about the agenda for the first meeting of the BACUP Steering Committee, scheduled to take place on 3rd December. Thereafter her diary is full of references to meetings and visits connected with BACUP work.

This first meeting of the Steering Committee would be crucial to the future of BACUP. Vicky had generated a tidal wave of enthusiasm and support at the October meeting which could not now be allowed to dissipate into inaction or be sidetracked by futile discourses or fruitless projects. She intended to put all her energies and rapidly burgeoning organizational skills at the disposal of BACUP but, impressive though they might be, they were not inexhaustible. This she knew better than anyone, just as she also knew that time was not on her side. Vicky did not have a moment to waste and no one working with her from that day forward would ever be allowed to forget these pressures. But, although time might be tight and resources might be limited, she would not allow these constraints to be an excuse for cutting corners. Everything to do with this project had to be as good as it possibly could be: every move towards ultimate realization had to be sharply focused and thought through to the last detail. This was the approach Vicky had always adopted for every previous project in her life and, since she was constitutionally incapable of producing slipshod work or behaving in an unprofessional manner, BACUP would have to be created in the same mould.

After the meeting was over, Vicky felt a strong sense of anti-climax. She had picked up certain tensions among the participants and wondered whether she was going to be able to hold the group together. Politics again! Just when she thought she had left all that behind in her first life. Reading the minutes, however, one can only marvel at the amount of ground she had managed to cover in the short period available to her between the two meetings, a fact made more remarkable when one remembers that she had been contending with operations and illness for much of the time.

Before the end of the year many of the action targets on that December agenda had been achieved. Yvonne Terry was formally appointed as the Project Co-ordinator for the Cancer Information Service and took up her post on 1st January 1985. Other staff requirements had been formulated, the most pressing one being a personal assistant for Vicky. Clare Mouat was appointed in mid-January. Sources of funds and gifts in kind like office equipment and computers were beginning to be located, many through influential contacts among the Steering Committee members. Deciding on the BACUP logo design and ordering official stationery were deemed to be top priority, closely followed by the need to orchestrate a carefully planned publicity campaign gearing up for the October launch.

Possibly the most astounding achievement was to have found suitable office accommodation, close to Barts, just as Vicky had wanted. Even before the meeting she had been trundling round Smithfield in her wheelchair, taking the opportunity between medical appointments to look at various properties. Now on December 13th she looked at three more in the area and decided that 121 Charterhouse Street was the best. It was only one floor in a poky, somewhat rundown house but it belonged to the Special Trustees of St Bartholomew's Hospital and they offered BACUP a ten-year lease on very favourable terms.

BACUP would place one year's rent (£3,875) on deposit which would be held for the duration of the lease to safeguard the trustees from any loss should the organization go broke in the meantime. At the end of the term the accrued interest would be given to BACUP. This was a mark of kindly prudence, given that the organization hardly existed and could boast no financial track record whatsoever. With the other hand, however, the Special Trustees showed their charitable heart, by donating a full year's lease to BACUP.

The Vicky charm had worked again. She had visited Sir Robin Brook, Chairman of the Trustees, at his home in Maida Vale. He had listened to her tale and after explaining that her kind of organization was not usually regarded as a good risk, told her that they would, however, be making an exception in her case because of who she was, the nature of the project and the calibre of the backers she had already mustered. He thoroughly approved the concept; even more, the person behind it.

At the least serious time of the year when most people are working themselves into a lather about Christmas or making fools of themselves at office parties, Vicky was rushing hither and yon from one appointment to the next, following up introductions, meeting City magnates and, wherever she went, explaining and selling BACUP. At home, she would spend many more hours on the telephone and writing letters. She never passed up a good opportunity to describe what she was about and eventually her persistence reaped handsome dividends. People were moved by her story and impressed by her personality. Vicky had an amazing capacity to make people believe in her and convince them that she could make it happen.

'An interesting thing about BACUP was the way it just started,' recalled Professor Ken Calman, who was to become one of BACUP's first trustees. 'It was great fun and very exciting to be involved from the beginning and see it move forward so rapidly but it was not surprising. She had such a persuasive personality.'

Vicky had been particularly pleased to win his support

because, as she soon discovered from their many conversations, they shared very similar views about information dissemination. Professor Calman also had some invaluable experience to impart to the fledgling organization: he had set up and for a while been closely associated with a similar small-scale operation in Glasgow called Tak Tent which means 'take care' in Glaswegian.

The excitement was intense and, at times, it all became too much. Then she would confide to her diary or to David that the pressures were overwhelming. He, as a good friend who obviously felt concerned about her health but also worried that she might get too carried away by the whole thing, saw it as necessary to try and talk her down occasionally. Vicky could be quite childish in her delight at the attention she was beginning to attract. Obviously, he was pleased for her but he did not want it to go to her head. He was her closest friend and he saw it as his duty to be ever present at her side as a touchstone to reality. Vicky was too practical and earth-based a person to indulge in wild fantasies but there was always the risk that physically she would run herself into the ground. As it was, her current activities were peaking at levels far beyond those that most healthy people in the prime of life would want or even be able to attempt. As time went on and Vicky defied ever more dire prognoses, it would become apparent that her physical endeavours were fuelled by little more than pure spirit.

On 28th December Vicky wrote a resumé of the rationale for setting up BACUP, the background research she had done so far and the plans for the future. She was now able to state confidently that the Cancer Information Service would be launched in the autumn of 1985 with four trained cancer nurses on the switchboard who would be backed up by leading medical and nursing specialists in oncology. Quite apart from the private donations she had received so far (the major portion coming from her parents), she was able to announce two highly successful fund-raising events organized by members at her erstwhile place of work. A sponsored walk across the South Downs which her former colleague Sue Jackson from the department of chemical endocrinology in Barts had stage-managed had raised £1,300. And a bottle of champagne raffled at Professor Lesley Rees's annual dinner for the same department went for £175. It was a sparkling send-off for BACUP into the new year of 1985.

Vicky and Tim spent Christmas at the cottage and the New Year in Sicily. As soon as they returned on 5th January Vicky plunged into work on BACUP, turning their Clapham house into the temporary headquarters. Clare Mouat worked in the dining room, Vicky was in her bedroom on the next floor and Yvonne Terry was on the floor above. Susie was down in the basement preparing meals and bringing them up on trays which she brought in without a word and later removed as silently, endeavouring not to interrupt what was going on. Betty came up from East Grinstead to lend a hand whenever she could. Papers were scattered everywhere and the telephones never stopped ringing. Visitors called to see Vicky on BACUP business, some taking more time than she could spare. In between times she taught Yvonne and Clare how to use the BBC computer, a skill she had only just acquired herself. A note of surrealism crept into the whole scenario when she found herself talking to the police about stolen money, a stressful situation which had been going on for some months and was connected with the family of a woman who had been cleaning for her. 'This place is Piccadilly' she groaned to her diary, and complained how hard it was to get the rest she needed so badly.

Hardly had the new regime begun to settle down than Vicky was back in hospital for another attempt with the monoclonal antibodies treatment. She dreaded it: for the pain she knew she would have and for a repetition of the unsympathetic nursing she had found so hard to take last time. In the event both turned out to be worse than she had anticipated. She spent one whole night leaking peritoneal fluid into her bed but the nurse refused to come near her because she said Vicky was radioactive. Another refused to bring her a commode, and when Vicky complained of pain, responded in a tone tinged with disbelief, as if to suggest she were malingering: 'Pain? What pain?' At the end of it all, and after two operations leaving her with a wound which had to be dressed twice daily by the district nurse for some time after she returned home, Vicky was told that the treatment had not worked and they could not try it again.

She was very upset by this information. Maurice Slevin consoled her, saying that she had been very brave. She could not afford to let the failure prey on her mind. Maurice was certain to come up with something new and meanwhile there was so much to do but always, as she told Yvonne more than once, so little time. From now on, with every new bout of treatment Vicky would be jolted up against the harsh reality — fully comprehended by her — that the cancer she had once hoped to conquer had returned and now taken up its permanent abode in her body. It was no longer a question of 'Have we got rid of it all?' but rather, 'How much time before the next advance strikes and when it does, how do we fight it?'

Vicky trusted her doctors totally, and Maurice quite especially. She knew she could rely on him to suggest any new avenues of treatment he thought might be beneficial. All the same, in early February she felt compelled to have a long chat with him about her future. She confessed that since the failure of the monoclonal antibodies therapy she no longer felt so confident about her treatment options. She questioned the value of further chemotherapy unless he could assure her that there would be benefits. Vicky must have known, even as she said this, that this was placing an unfair burden of responsibility on him but it worried her that her quality of life might become severely impaired if she had to submit to many more of these gruelling sessions. Her suffering would only be worthwhile if she remained fit enough to pursue the business of BACUP.

Such a defeatist tone was uncharacteristic of Vicky, and, as it later turned out, only momentary, but it can perhaps be partially explained by the stress she was under to meet her targets on BACUP, combined with the fact that all around her it seemed that her friends were losing out to cancer. Linda Powers in America was deteriorating rapidly. Valerie Mann, who was a fellow patient in Barts, had just been told that no further treatment was possible. A little later (and, for Vicky, saddest news of all), she was very shocked to learn that on 3rd March her friend Bryan Skinner had died of pneumonia, a final complication of his cancer. She had come to know him and his wife Celia very well since their first conversation in June last year. She had stayed with them in their beautiful house in Jersey several times to discuss the formation and future of BACUP and she had very much valued his advice, following it to the letter in many respects and consulting him at every point. He had also been instrumental in introducing her to many prominent people in industry and the City. So now she wrote in her diary: 'Can't believe he's gone – so sad he is not here to see BACUP take off – I have so much to tell him and he would have loved to see BACUP become a reality – in many ways I wouldn't be doing this if not for him . . . we must keep our chins up – work must go on.'

There was so much to do if they were to achieve the launch objective of October 31st.

Ken Calman had visited her in hospital to help her finalize

the BACUP application to the Cancer Research Campaign (CRC) for a grant to evaluate the information service. Getting this right had entailed several drafts and special deliveries but she managed to submit it just in time, and a sum of £5,000 was approved at the meeting of the CRC education committee in February. Another triumph for BACUP (Vicky really) was to be a prizewinner in *The Guardian* computer competition, receiving a Digital Rainbow 100 Computer, estimated to be worth about £4,000.

In February, Yvonne Terry had spent three weeks in New York observing the work of the American cancer information service and receiving a training from the National Cancer Institute which was the funding organization. She came back even more enthused by the project and started collating information and writing up preparatory material for the leaflets.

More staff were appointed. Dr Sheila Jones, a retired lecturer in psychology, was seconded on a voluntary basis from an organization for retired executives called REACH. Her job was to help set up a pilot study to evaluate the Cancer Information Service. From National Westminster Enterprises (a scheme run by NatWest to help small businesses and charities) came Bob Kennerley-Tayler who was to help with general office administration for two years on a full-time basis, his salary being paid by NatWest. Carol St Ledger, a psychology graduate, was appointed to help Yvonne develop the resource material for the Cancer Information Service.

In May the BACUP staff moved into the third floor of 121 Charterhouse Street. The premises had been completely renovated: cloakrooms and kitchens were installed, partitions put up, walls painted, curtains hung and office furniture brought in, much of it donated. The entire refurbishment was done free of charge by the John Brunton partnership of architects and the building contractors, Higgs & Hill. British Telecom installed the switchboard and a computerized telephone system, also for no payment.

These generous gifts to BACUP which represented something in the region of £50,000 had been organized by another
of Vicky's admirers. Michael Miskin, a retired property de-
veloper, had recently been introduced to Vicky by their mutual
friend, Dr Peter Wrigley. Like so many others before and after
him, he was immediately captivated by this 'incredible individual – she was nothing less than a phenomenon'. The
piquant flavour of his first encounter with Vicky is worth
recounting because it was an experience many others shared
with him, including myself. Vicky had a low-pitched, resonant
voice, the clarity of which was emphasized by her articulate
delivery. Her bravura performance on the video she had made
for the College of Health showed to what good effect she
could put it.

'Hearing her speak on the telephone,' said Mr Miskin, 'I had
expected to meet a tall, willowy, blonde English type, so what
a surprise to open my door to this little Oriental lady. I
looked at her CV and I was amazed. All those papers she had
written, prizes she had won, learned societies to which she
belonged! I was immediately fascinated by her as an individual
and when she explained what she was doing I just wanted to
do everything I could to help her.'

And so he did. Not only did he manage to organize these
gifts in kind but he also gave her advice on negotiating the
first lease so that she could have an option on further space in
the building which the Steering Committee anticipated would
soon be needed. As it was, their quarters were very cramped.
Clare Mouat remembered that she had to 'hurdle over her
desk and then just stay, sealed there'. Vicky, never inclined to
let anything slip out of her control, took a close personal
interest in the design of the offices and brought a few bits and
pieces of her own from Northbourne Road, including an old
sofa which is still there today in the office of the fund-
raising manager, somewhat decrepid but still serviceable. Many

people remember Vicky sitting or lying on that sofa; she would be sparking away, throwing off ideas, reviewing plans, dictating letters or just resting as she prepared herself for yet another meeting or media interview.

All the while intense work was being put into developing the information service. Fact sheets on the more common cancers such as breast and lung cancer were being written and checked for accuracy by specialist doctors with the purpose of sending them off to enquirers who asked for more detailed information than could be given on the telephone. Maurice Slevin had already written, with two colleagues, a booklet, *Diet and the Cancer Patient*, which was sponsored by Sainsbury's and the first to be published in the now well-known BACUP 'Understanding Cancer' series. Vicky herself wrote the first draft of *Coping with Hair Loss*, a subject about which she never ceased to feel passionately. The final version, as it appears today, is almost as Vicky wrote it. She knew how important it was to share the practical hints like, for instance, not getting too close to an open oven door with an acrylic wig which can all too easily frizzle. This was a tip passed on to her by Celia Skinner, the widow of Bryan, her businessman friend, who is herself a cancer survivor. Today, Mrs Skinner is the President of Jersey BACUP, the first and so far the only one of BACUP's regional contact points.

The response manual containing commonly asked questions about cancer was being compiled by the medical and specialist advisory board. Yvonne and Carol were putting together a resource directory containing information about other organizations, support groups and services. Both were intended for the nurses to use. Yvonne went on a two-day training course in telephone communication techniques. The call record form was being continually refined. The guidelines for the nurses' telephone responses – the manner, method and content – were also constantly under discussion between Vicky, Yvonne and Maurice.

From the beginning, Vicky had always been very emphatic that BACUP should not be regarded as a threat of any kind to the medical profession. It was to be expected that many of the people ringing in would be seeking information they felt had been denied to them by their own doctors but the nurses must never be seen as either intruding on or questioning that relationship. Whatever callers might say to them, or ask of them, they must not be tempted into giving a prognosis and they were always to encourage patients to go back to their own doctors. She wanted the service to be seen as primarily an information service, strongly backed by its medical advisers to whom the nurses, in cases of difficulty, would have swift and easy access. Even Vicky, with all her experience of being a patient and hearing what other patients had to say, did not anticipate the profound depths of emotional need that this service would stir up.

A remarkable progress report was presented to the second BACUP Working Party meeting on 19th June 1985. Present were most of those people who had been invited to the first meeting in October 1984 as well as some new faces. After BACUP was formally launched, this group was to form the nucleus of people invited by Vicky to become a Founder Friend of BACUP. Later still, she hit on the idea of having Celebrity Friends as well. Well-known personalities like Dirk Bogarde, Felicity Kendall and Clare Rayner were delighted to accept Vicky's invitation and today there are many more Celebrity Friends who willingly lend their name and presence to fund-raising events for BACUP.

At that meeting there were several important developments to report. A firm of professional fund-raisers had been appointed on a year's contract. Meanwhile, more grant applications were being submitted to, among others, the Big Four of the cancer organizations: the Cancer Research Campaign; the Imperial Cancer Research Fund; the Marie Curie Memorial

Foundation and the National Society for Cancer Relief. In the fullness of time, all were to respond generously. The trustees of Bryan Skinner's estate had promised £50,000 and his company, Crest Nicholson, a further £20,000. His widow, showing considerable magnanimity, refused Vicky's offer of turning the gift into a Bryan Skinner Memorial Fellowship because she felt it was important that BACUP should have maximum freedom at this early stage to use its money in whatever way it felt was most appropriate. Dame Mary Donaldson agreed to be President of BACUP.

Finally, very excitingly, BACUP was to run a pilot cancer information service in two districts in the South West Thames area in September, a month before the launch proper. This mini-service would enable Yvonne, Vicky and Maurice to form some idea of the sort of calls they ought to expect in the future and give them a chance to iron out any wrinkles in the call record form or the system generally. The response to that trial service was very encouraging although somewhat daunting. The telephones rang constantly. Yvonne, assisted by Cecile Messent, the first of the team of cancer nurses to be employed by BACUP, began to get a foretaste of the overwhelming need out there. A second nurse, Sue Chambers, who joined them at the beginning of October recalls how exciting it was but also how demanding. 'You no sooner put the phone down than it would ring again.' In those weeks before the launch the nurses learnt some basic techniques for answering the calls. They also realized that it was not just information many people were seeking, but emotional support. They wondered if they would be able to cope.

BACUP was ready to go. The time had come to move into top gear the publicity machine which Peter Belchamber, a public relations expert, had been so carefully priming for the past few months. He had planned the strategy, in detail with Vicky, and also with his Public Relations committee, whose members all had media expertise in one form or another. They were agreed that it was important to raise awareness of BACUP without saturating the public mind or, fatally, turning editors and programme-makers off the idea before it had even happened because 'we've done that already'.

A few judiciously placed interviews in various newspapers and specialist journals in the spring led to major features in two quality newspapers in September. Dame Mary Donaldson was an invaluable ally because, after her year as the first woman Lord Mayor of London, she continued to maintain a high public profile and was now willing to talk about her experience of breast cancer some years previously which had involved her having a bilateral mastectomy (both breasts removed).

Then there was Vicky's radio interview with Professor Anthony Clare in his series *In the Psychiatrist's Chair*. It was broadcast on 21st July but it had in fact been recorded on 9th April and in the run-up beforehand, indeed ever since Anthony Clare had made the suggestion after the October meeting, the prospect had caused Vicky much private concern. She was extremely flattered to have been invited to do the interview and, with her instinctive nose for what was good publicity, she knew that it would be an excellent opportunity for promoting BACUP. She did not mind sharing her experiences so publicly. At the same time the little girl who still lingered in her worried about what her parents would say when they heard her views on God. She had had several painful discussions with her friend David about it.

He was not so happy about her doing this interview because he felt that Vicky was in danger of putting herself into an intolerable position: she might feel compelled to expose more of herself than she wished; alternatively, she might not be true to herself because she might conceal certain things for fear of hurting some of her dearest friends. Vicky was one of those unusual creatures – an extrovert introvert – so although on the whole she gave the impression of being very outgoing, inside she was deeply reflective about everything she did. Even after the interview was over, she continued to worry and go over it in her mind. Only when the letters started to flood in, some of which brought tears to her eyes, and her friends could reassure her quite sincerely that she had done very well, did she begin to relax.

She had listened to that broadcast lying in her bed at the Royal Marsden Hospital which she had entered shortly after the second Working Party meeting. There she had spent a month enduring a particularly traumatic and dangerous treatment involving high doses of chemotherapy (Meltholan) and bone marrow transplantation. It was highly experimental, and life-threatening because of the risk of infection, so she was isolated from the other patients. No one really knew what the results would be but that did not deter Vicky. Her fighting spirit was back in full strength, never again to leave her. She had told Maurice that she wanted to be alive for the launch of BACUP in October and she was determined to achieve that goal. It was one of Vicky's ways of coping: to set herself short-term objectives and then concentrate all her energies on meeting them.

'I didn't think about death very much at the time,' she later told me. 'It was tough enough just getting through the treatment.'

The side effects were distressing. Hair loss she was prepared for and could cope with, having now acquired a variety of head pieces to choose from, including a towelling turban. What she did find very difficult to endure was the effect the chemotherapy had on her gums and buccal mucous membrane. It made her mouth very sore, dry and swollen. She was also more nauseated than she could ever remember. The nausea and vomiting continued after she returned home, so in desperation she enlisted the services of a hypnotherapist, a friend of Maurice, who did make her feel better. He invited her to imagine going down an escalator into her garden whereupon, as she records in her diary, she burst into tears: 'in fact twice – I suppose my garden represents my life and I thought I might never get home to it and I'm crying for suffering I've had'.

Slowly, the warm summer days and the company of friends helped her to recover. She had been dictating letters and doing a lot of work even in hospital and by the end of July BACUP business was occupying all of her time. The rushing around started again. On 1st August she interviewed candidates for the Cancer Information Service with Tim McElwain, Maurice Slevin and Richard Wells, a senior oncology nurse, at the Royal Marsden Hospital. This was when Cecile Messent and Sue Chambers were appointed.

In the middle of August she and Tim took a much needed holiday. They spent a marvellous week in Marbella where they had a hotel demi-suite with their own garden. Every morning they would breakfast late on the balcony; Vicky would feed the stray cats – against her better judgement – but she found them irresistible; the rest of the day she would swim and sunbathe, even play a few games of tables tennis and walk on the sand. She shouted at their noisy German neighbour who was conducting his business affairs over the telephone to be quiet. She loved the social life: eating delicious buffet lunches at the side of the pool (her appetite was coming back slowly); and she enjoyed watching the other guests in the dining room at night. She had had a short break earlier in the year in Brittany with David and it was then she had first swum with her colostomy. She wore now the same bikini top and shorts that she had bought for that holiday. Sometimes in the early evening when the beach was deserted she even swam topless. It was a memorable holiday but all too short.

Vicky returned to a hive of activity. She was delighted to hear how well the pilot survey was going. Countless letters had to be written. She was punctilious about thanking people for the smallest service or gift they might offer and when it was a matter of answering cancer-related letters, she put an immense amount of care and thought and genuine empathy into each of her answers. Later, when the service was in full swing, Vicky would take personal responsibility for devising the answers. People would often write in detail about their own or a relative's cancer experience, so Vicky always made a point of devoting at least a paragraph to that human story before giving the correspondent the useful practical information they needed.

She was writing an article for the 'Personal View' section of the *British Medical Journal* which was timed to appear a couple of weeks before the launch. It was called 'Cancer and beyond: the formation of BACUP' and Vicky spent a week working on it and worrying about it. Countless drafts were written and read by friends who suggested additions and subtractions. Maurice said it needed more emotions and she cried over the word processor as she wrote about her recurrence. Twice in a year she had had to reveal so much of her inner self to the world – first with Anthony Clare and now in this article addressed to her own profession – but it was crucial that she should capture the interest and support of GPs and hospital doctors. She needed their cooperation and support in the tripartite partnership she aimed to create between patients, their relatives and friends and the health professionals. At the end of the week she was able to meet Tim at the airport with a final version. He read it and pronounced it to be 'great, like a thriller' and she was relieved and delighted, recording in her diary: 'I feel so much better.'

The article was accompanied by a four-page illustrated insert explaining what BACUP was, who was behind it and how the service would be run. The expense of printing and producing 85,000 of these leaflets was donated by Robert Maxwell, the publisher.

In the weeks approaching the launch the media began to wake up to the notion that they might have a good story on their hands. Requests for interviews were coming in thick and fast.

'Vicky was very attractive to the media,' said Peter Belchamber who was masterminding the operation with immaculate precision and foresight. 'She had all this drive and enthusiasm and she was so lucid and committed. She was also intriguing, a bit different and, of course, not a bit shy.'

The official launch, accompanied by a press conference for medical journalists, took place on Thursday, 31st October 1985. The whole thing ran like clockwork. There were seven television spots on five different channels, including an item on *Newsnight* the previous evening. There were also several radio reports and interviews and wide press coverage. It was a case of picking the best, not scratching around for what might come up. They were able, for instance, to make the luxurious decision that Vicky would not accept an invitation to appear on breakfast television.

'We thought it would spoil the mood for the rest of the day,' Vicky said. 'I think we were right. We hit the jackpot.'

Vicky performed brilliantly. She was filmed walking with sprightly gait to the BACUP offices in Charterhouse Street. She was shown in her garden; playing the piano; talking with Tim in their home; listening to the nurses. Sometimes she was wearing her trilby hat; at other times she was shown bareheaded and close-cropped. No doubt about it. A star was born. And she clearly loved every moment of it.

The press conference was equally successful. There was an impressive line-up of speakers who each highlighted key points about BACUP. They included Stephen Gold, a cancer survivor and member of the executive, who talked movingly from his own experience about the need for an organization like BACUP. It would give others like him the information they so often desperately needed as well as a chance to share their feelings with a sympathetic listener and so break out of that 'cancer closet' Vicky hated so much.

Hardened journalists went away saying they couldn't remember when they had attended such a well-organized press do. BACUP never saw a bill. Like so many others, the Charles Barker organization, and Peter Belchamber in particular, had freely donated their expertise, premises, office facilities and countless other gifts in kind. Above all their expensive time. Favourable articles were written and the BACUP lines started ringing.

Vicky had written in her *BMJ* article that she had survived her experiences and that she now remained well 'with a window of hope for the future'. She believed her own words and with good reason. She was a survivor and now, once more, the horizon seemed to be stretching away, if not indefinitely, at least into an indiscernible distance.

14

BACUP:
The Dream Comes True

❖

O N SATURDAY, 16th November 1985 Vicky and Tim held a party at their house in Northbourne Road to celebrate the launch of BACUP. It was a crowded affair with people in rooms on every floor and sitting out on the stairs to eat their supper. Vicky was darting hither and thither, with special words that really did mean something for each guest. Later she sat at the piano and played duets with David – Scott Joplin and favourites like 'Stormy Weather' and 'Look for the Silver Lining'.

Everyone there had had some part to play in the creation of BACUP. Whether great or small, she wanted to acknowledge their contribution and this was her very personal way of showing her appreciation. It was one of those occasions no one present will ever forget: at once a triumph and a tragedy. There was an immense poignancy about the slight, animated figure, with her round shaven head and her eyes sparkling with pleasure and delight, moving along her friends and well-wishers. Vicky always enjoyed a good party and here it was, all happening and all these people here in her house, acclaiming her because of BACUP, the dream she had dared to dream and make come true. The life force surging from her that evening was so palpable it seemed a monstrous, wicked lie to think she was suffering from a disease which already had her firmly in its grasp.

Indeed, it was quite amazing that Vicky managed even to be present at her own party. After the excitement of the launch and before she had had much time to savour the response, which was overwhelming, she began once more to experience severe abdominal pain and vomiting. She staggered through the days, forcing herself into the office as often as possible because she wanted to see how the nurses were coping with the demand and what needed to be done to support them. Naturally, everyone had hoped and prayed for a good response but probably not even Vicky, who knew more than most about the great unmet need out there, could have foreseen just how huge it would be.

The telephones rang ceaselessly and the letters were coming in at the rate of forty a day. Many recounted a tale of human misery and despair. Here are just a few examples from that huge postbag.

The woman with breast cancer, for example, who took two years to convince her consultant that she had a breast lump which needed attention. When finally she was admitted for an operation she awoke to find that without advance discussion she had been given a full radical mastectomy. 'When the consultant came round,' she wrote to Vicky, 'I said to him "I did have a lump", and all he replied was "Oh, it was only the size of a ten p piece". I have a scar from what was under my arm to my waist. From that day I have lost all faith in doctors and I just wish men could experience the worry and pain and after effects . . . much more must be done to advise GPs and consultants to take a woman seriously even if it's a false alarm.'

There was the thirty-year-old married man with three young children who had had a massive operation for cancer of the oesophagus six months earlier and thanked Vicky for letting him vent his feelings. 'Cancer! Me! Why me! Why not Joe

Bloggs down the road? Not me. I cried a lot and so did my wife ... My friends have been good to me but even they could not clear the *terrible* fears I had in my mind ... I cram all I can into every day as maybe there won't be another chance tomorrow.'

A man wrote about his personal experience of 'the absolute devastation cancer can cause within families, and the over-whelming sense of helplessness one feels as a relative of a cancer victim'. He felt that if BACUP had been in existence when he needed it he would have been more supportive and understanding to members of his own family with cancer. Like many others, he enclosed a small donation with his letter.

A woman who had nursed her husband through cancer to his death echoed and expanded this view. She said that she and her husband 'knew every step of the way what was happening, why it was happening and what the prognosis was. This was very hard to take at times, but we would have had it no other way.' She too welcomed BACUP because she had been in the situation 'where the truth has been hidden from the patient with cancer, and this seems not only wrong but inhumane; making a lie of an entire family and friends' relationships at the time when the utmost love, support, com-passion and care are required. Reassurance too can be given confidently when backed by truth, and taken in trust'. How much Vicky agreed with those sentiments! That was exactly what she intended BACUP should offer to all who called upon its services.

Not all were stories of despair. Many were uplifting and encouraging and almost invariably enthusiastically supportive of BACUP. A recently bereaved widower described his wife's six years of living with breast cancer as being, 'in spite of all the problems, the most *rewarding* of our *twenty-three* years together. It is clear,' he went on, 'that you are a lady of great courage and perspicacity, and that there are no platitudes I can offer you as a comfort. By her [his wife's] example, however, I can tell you that Audrey has removed my own fear of death and dying. When I recall her last few weeks, what had to be done and what can happen. I can say with certainty that there *are* worse things than death and that sometimes it comes as a friend.'

Doctors and nurses also wrote to Vicky, delighted that she should be helping them in their work. One wrote: 'You touch the heart of the matter when you say "communication was a key to overcome problems". The doctor-patient relationship is rightly changing and the patient, as the consumer, should have much more information provided.' For Vicky to have support coming from this quarter, her own profession, was particularly heartwarming. It made her feel more than ever confirmed in the decision she had made a year ago to go ahead with BACUP, whatever the personal cost to her. She knew that once she had the doctors on her side BACUP would survive, even if she herself could not live to see all its triumphs.

Vicky took care to answer each one of these letters with sympathy as well as accurate information. Where required, leaflets were enclosed, addresses of support groups or other organizations supplied and always, there was the genuine personal note of interest underlined by Vicky's own signature – Chairman and Honorary Director. She would take the letters home with her or into the hospital and dictate her answers to Clare Mouat from her bedside. She was to become a familiar sight to her visitors and the medical staff in both Barts and the Homerton Hospital, lying in a bed covered with papers, scribbling notes, dictating into her tape recorder or talking BACUP business on the telephone.

'Now I know it's not only President Reagan who can run a country from his bedside,' said Professor Chris Williams after one of his visits.

Despite all these concerns, Vicky always remained keenly interested in her friends and what they were doing. One woman recalls that she would ring Vicky from time to time and Vicky would always ask about her and her family — 'genuinely, she cared'. She would also expand with great enthusiasm about the latest development with BACUP but 'she never whinged on about what was happening to her, like most of us would, especially in that kind of situation. She was never self-pitying.' Vicky wanted to keep her finger on BACUP's pulse all the time. She was determined that it should be a streamlined first-class service. She could not abide ineffectual or amateurish efforts in anything and this made her a tough task master — on herself first and foremost but on everyone else as well. She was quicksilver mentally and physically: sharp at assessing a problem and deft in executing its solution. She found it hard to understand how other people could think and act so much more slowly. She controlled her impatience for the most part but there were times when she found it intolerable and she would release a wounding comment. A natural autocrat, she also never lost the instincts and habits of her former life when, as a rigorous researcher, she could never quite bring herself to trust anyone else to do the job as well as her. If it had been humanly possible, Vicky would have done everything in BACUP herself but that, of course, was out of the question.

Vicky had learnt a tremendous amount in the last year. She had proved to be an organizer and a motivator, a propagandist and a good publicist for her cause, but some of the more subtle skills of management eluded her. She was a leader — no question of that — but what she lacked was the time to spend with individual members of staff, listen to their problems and sort out the inevitable personality clashes that are bound to occur in a new organization where everyone and everything is untried. She was aware of these lacks in herself and being Vicky, had she had a little more time and a little less illness, she would undoubtedly have made it her business to acquire these useful teambuilding skills.

But her priority was BACUP. Now that she had given birth to her idea, with the skilled assistance of people like Yvonne Terry and all the volunteers in the background, she had to give her precious offspring everything she could to be sure that it grew up into the right kind of association, a service dedicated to helping others. She did not want it to degenerate into one of those self-serving organizations which seem to exist mainly for those who work in them.

The inevitable strains on everyone working at full stretch had been beginning to show, even before the launch, and now, as BACUP was swinging into top speed, it was clearly vital to appoint a full-time administrator. At the beginning of November Vicky had a long talk with Richard Driscoll who was then the social administrator of the Renal Unit at Barts. They liked each other and Richard was duly offered the post of Administrator which he took up in February 1986 and still occupies today. The nurses were given training in communication skills by trainer, Ivan Sokolov, and gradually other appointments were made: a librarian, a research officer, two more nurses and a couple of volunteers who came in on a regular basis to help in the office.

The organization was growing apace. By the time the first issue of *BACUP News* was published in April 1986 there was a full-time staff of eleven and yearly running costs were estimated to be £250,000, three quarters of which had to be found from voluntary contributions.

The newspaper had always been one of Vicky's pet projects and the story of how it came into being is a good example of the way she refused to be thwarted when she had set her heart on something. In the early days when she was still canvassing support for her concept of BACUP she would invariably, at some stage in the discussion, flourish a copy of *Balance* the magazine of the British Diabetic Association, and say, if diabetics can have their own association and a magazine that looks as good as this, why not cancer patients? She intended the BACUP newspaper to be written primarily with patients in mind. It would be their forum, providing them with an opportunity to exchange experiences, pool knowledge, learn from each other and hear about developments in cancer and new treatments. She found a freelance medical journalist, Jenny Bryan, who was enthusiastic about the idea and produced costings. For some time the Executive resisted the proposal because they felt it was an expensive item in the budget and there was not much evidence to suggest that it would pay its way by bringing in donations.

Vicky refused to budge. If the Executive would not agree an allocation of money, she would find an alternative source. Back she went to her father who had already dipped deep into his pocket for BACUP (and continues to do so to this day). He gave her the £30,000 she needed and the newspaper was on its way. Today in its fourth year of existence the immediate future of *BACUP News* has been secured by a generous offer of further four-year funding from the Worshipful Company of Leathersellers.

Vicky was justified in her persistence. The newspaper is lively, readable, professionally laid out and produced. It comes out three times a year and still follows her original format and intention. The front page usually carries one or two articles about controversial developments in cancer treatment and BACUP events, especially when they involve celebrities. The centre pages are devoted to readers' experiences. For example, in one recent issue a teenager describes what it is like to lose all your hair and have months of intensive chemotherapy for a rare tumour of the spine. 'The worst thing you can say to someone who is being treated for cancer is "I know what you're going through,"' she says. The reality for her and for others in her situation is that she feels angry at the unfairness of life, jealous that her friends have been spared all the pain and misery, and frightened about her future. But she is also optimistic and determined to beat her illness. In another issue a grandfather writes in a droll way about his undignified experiences with tests and then treatment for bowel cancer. Readers' letters are given a full page. This is their chance to express views and share problems or pass on useful tips. Other regular features include stories about fund-raising events, book reviews, up-dates on other cancer help organizations and, invariably, at least one in-depth article about a new treatment for a particular cancer. There is not a hint of talking down or patronizing people with cancer. No suggestion that cancer turns you into a helpless victim. The tone is upbeat and realistic – like its begetter.

'Well we did it! It has been a tremendous year . . .' she started her Chairman's letter on the front page of the first issue. The colour picture at the head of the column shows Vicky with a big grin, sporting a red spotted bow tie on a striped man's shirt and, of course, her by now famous grey trilby hat. She was talking about BACUP, naturally, and its astonishing growth in six months. It was currently helping more than 300 families a week.

Few of her readers could have guessed what a bad year it had been so far for Vicky. Hardly had she returned from her Christmas holiday with Tim on the island of Mustique when, on 2nd January, she was whisked into hospital with an obstruction in her gut. She had been having problems ever since November and the food and windy climate in Mustique had only served to aggravate her discomfort. Now she became seriously ill, so ill indeed that even Maurice, who had always before been able to come up with a new suggestion, felt that there was nothing more he could offer her. The cancer had come back and was blocking her bowels and kidneys. She had tubes everywhere and she also had pneumonia. Maurice felt 'extremely sad and desperate for her' but when he looked at her condition and asked himself whether he would wish for himself or any member of his family to continue living in such a state, the answer was no. It seemed the time had come for Vicky to give up the struggle and resign herself to accepting death. Surely she would feel the same. However, the answer he received when he spoke to Vicky and Tim together was quite different.

Although she was near death, Vicky's mind remained quite lucid. Was there really nothing else? she asked him. Only some hormonal treatment which occasionally worked, he responded, but that would be for a limited period and eventually she would be back to all her tubes and bags that were now draining her bodily fluids. Let me have it, was her immediate request.

This was the only time in their relationship where there was a serious rift between them. Vicky was frosty for weeks and she was also uncharacteristically impatient with the nurses and doctors. Maurice believes that this behaviour was Vicky's way of expressing the very understandable anger she felt at the advance of the disease. Up to now she had always been able to surmount the problems: another drastic operation, another punishing dose of chemotherapy but she always bounced back. In all these brave exploits Maurice had been her collaborator and her supporter. Now she felt betrayed by his withdrawal and she transferred her anger at her helplessness to him. Neither then, nor later did she ask for sympathy. Give me the treatment, she said, and whatever happens, if it helps me live a few months longer, then it will have been worth it.

He felt very unhappy that he had caused her this distress and had apparently let her down by misunderstanding so completely what she wanted for herself. However, in time to come, he was glad that he had had this discussion with Vicky because he knew that whatever he did thenceforward to cope with her problems, he was doing it because she wanted it. There were some among his colleagues who were later to accuse him of 'grotesque management' of her disease and suggest that he had allowed himself to be manipulated by Vicky. Maurice has come out of this experience believing firmly that the decision when to stop treatment must at least be allowed to the patient. What is always problematic is when and how you present the opportunity because this is obviously the moment when the doctor has to tell the patient that the condition is terminal.

Vicky later used to say to her medical friends that had she more time she would have liked to write a paper on 'Life after terminal care diagnosis'. If there was anyone who could say something new and interesting on the subject it was Vicky. In the months to come she was to amaze and confound her carers and those who knew her well by the sheer number of her Houndini-like escapes from death. Eventually, she was to spend more of her time in than out of hospital but whenever she was out she lived every moment of her life with an extraordinary intensity and relish.

'Just give me a tiny inch and I will get pleasure out of it and it will pull me up,' she said to me, six weeks before she died.

Quality of life and what it meant in real everyday terms was very important to Vicky, and something about which she would often talk. She believed that the secret of achieving a good quality of life, even in the most adverse circumstances, lay in cultivating the art of the possible. She saw no virtue in hankering after pleasures and pursuits which had been possible to her in good health. That way lay futility and frustration. Ever rational, she decided that the only sensible way of dealing with her debilitating illness was to trim her expectations to match her abilities. There was no point in railing against the unkind fates; instead, by concentrating on what she could achieve she 'derived the greatest joy from the simplest of pleasures' like walking round her garden or going out to dinner with friends.

*

Although Vicky was determined to recover she had also accepted that she might not so, in February 1986, in her usual thorough way, she made careful preparations for her death. As Maurice Slevin observed, with some amazement, 'death became another project'. Again it was something which she and Tim did together. A nurse was organized to look after her at home, the GP was put on alert and she met the local Hospice team who would be responsible for keeping her pain under control. Tim typed out a list of her jewellery and Vicky made her will, bequeathing individual items of jewellery and other personal gifts to her family, her friends and each of their children, naming them all – a touching and entirely typical gesture. The far-flung Yip family was summoned to her bedside. Vicky said her goodbyes and everyone grieved around her. But when George walked in and asked, in an older brother kind of way, whether she would like to see a priest and give her instructions for her funeral service, she gave him short shrift. She was not ready to make that final step.

And then the miracle happened. Against all the odds, Vicky responded extraordinarily well to the new treatment. The tumour shrank to a third of its size and the kidney blockage cleared up. Her bowels, however, remained so severely obstructed that she could no longer take food by mouth.

For the remaining eighteen months of her life Vicky was drip-fed throughout the night from bags containing all the essential nutrients we need to keep us alive. The formula was made up for her by her friend Alison's husband, Michael Farthing (now Professor of gastroenterology). The bags were suspended at her bedside and injected through her Hickman line (the catheter inserted into her chest wall). This system of feeding is called total parenteral nutrition (TPN). Although some patients with non-malignant disease have been known to survive on it for several years, Vicky undoubtedly set a record for cancer patients. Even more remarkably, she did it as an out-patient a good deal of the time and even managed to travel abroad with all the paraphernalia. She went to Jersey twice and to Hong Kong, a very special visit home, in November 1986.

None of this would have been possible without the support and devotion that Tim and David gave her. At times it was very hard, admits Tim. They had said their goodbyes and done their mourning when she had been so near to death in February. They did not want her to die but their own lives were now completely subjugated to Vicky's needs. But they had their rewards too — the pleasure of seeing Vicky realize her ambitions for BACUP.

Vicky the foodie had, if anything, become more of a gourmand through the years of her cancer. She was wont to say: 'If I can only eat a bit, then it might as well be exquisite.' She loved trying out new restaurants, very often in the company of David, and her diary is peppered with references to menus and special meals. Now she was determined that this new affliction was not going to spoil one of her favourite pleasures so she devised her own quite unique method of dealing with the problem.

'Chewing and spitting' is what she called her new habit, a very precise description. She would take a mouthful of food, savour it in her mouth, chew it, enjoy the flavours and then, instead of swallowing it, spit it out discreetly on to a side plate. When her main plate was empty and the pile was high, she would cover it with a napkin. At the Waterside Inn she plucked a carnation from the vase to crown the pile. Her friends became quite used to this but, with perhaps more empathy than Vicky felt for fellow dinners, they would try to find a table in a corner where she could not be easily seen. At the Mirabelle the head waiter leant forward and said to David: 'Do not explain, Monsieur. We have all seen her on television and we think she is wonderful.' In this manner Vicky chewed and spat her way round all the best restaurants in London.

The other major problem with which she had to contend from this time forward was pain. Maurice asked Sister Jo Hockley, leader of the palliative care team at Barts, one of whose main tasks is to help terminally ill patients control their pain, to talk to Vicky about the need for diamorphine and explain how she could administer the dose herself. 'It is difficult to tell patients,' she said, 'because it's like saying it's the end. Obviously you have to be very careful what you say, otherwise you destroy their hope.'

Vicky found the information hard to take, as would anyone else finding themselves in the same circumstances but, true to character, her way of coping was to confront the situation, treating it as yet another challenge. She also had an advantage, compared to other patients, in that she was a doctor and could cope more easily with the equipment for giving herself the pain-killing injections which was contained in a box no bigger than a pencil case. She also had pain killers constantly pumping into her system through a battery-operated syringe driver. This is a needle inserted into the skin with a line leading into a small box containing the drugs. The box can be carried in an under-arm holster or in a pocket and the drug seeps through in a measured dose over a twenty-four-hour period. Towards the end of her life, Vicky was absorbing extremely high and almost continuous doses of these drugs (heroin and Buscopan) in order to control the pain.

Vicky had always been a sensual person. She enjoyed all the pleasures of the flesh but now she began to look on her body as a mere mechanical object, something that must be made to work at least enough to keep her going and get her around. She was living for BACUP rather than for herself, or even for those whom she loved most. BACUP was her creation; her pride; her joy; her life. In a very real sense she was BACUP and BACUP needed her still in order to become safely established. Vicky was not ready to die yet.

'You can do anything you like below the neck,' she said to Maurice. 'I don't care what you do to my body, provided my mind is o.k.'

In the spring and summer of 1986 Vicky was dreadfully frail but she managed to make two teaching videos for medical students, one with Anthony Clare with whom she had now struck up a close friendship. Although in considerable pain, which at moments she could not conceal, she was determined to give as much of herself as possible in these interviews because she felt it was so important to impress on students at the start of their medical careers that they should be aware of the emotional and psychological needs of their patients as well as being concerned for their physical treatment. These were the people who would carry on her message in their practice.

There is a moving moment in one of these videos where she urges the students to be willing to cry with their patients. Anthony Clare, as if not sure that he has really heard her words, asks her to repeat them which Vicky does with even more emphasis.

'What would you have said a few years ago before your illness if somebody had said that to you?' he asks.

'That it was very unprofessional,' replied Vicky, with a smile.

Most doctors would still think that to be the case but Vicky's example and that of others like her – Bernie Siegel, for instance, the American cancer surgeon and author of *Love, Medicine and Miracles* – is having a subtle influence. Some recent cancer patients have told me of their doctor holding their hand when they broke the bad news and perhaps even giving them a little hug.

At the end of June Vicky went to stay with her friends Jenny and James Dunlop in Stockport. They had organized a large fund-raising barbecue and dinner dance for BACUP. It was very hot weather and Jenny was shocked by Vicky's appearance when she arrived with Tim after a difficult journey, all her medicines and equipment in tow. She rested for three hours and then appeared at eleven o'clock in the evening to draw the raffle tickets and tell the assembled revellers about BACUP. As always she rose to the occasion and radiated enthusiasm. 'She's a one-off,' marvelled a guest.

Between bouts of illness Vicky continued to go into BACUP and, when she was too ill, she brought her work home, mainly those hundreds of letters that kept coming in. Many of the writers were now expressing their gratitude for what BACUP had done for them.

'Receiving information from BACUP is the single, most hopeful and encouraging thing that has happened to me since I was told I had cancer.'

'I am so glad that BACUP exists. It was a great relief to talk to someone who could answer my questions, and who was prepared to listen to my worries and give me reassurance.'

'I found it very difficult to put into words what I wanted to say but the nurse understood exactly how I felt. She made me feel wanted and not a nuisance.'

Some patients were so grateful for BACUP's help that they wanted to give something back. Mary Richards, for example, who, in a wheelchair, took part in a two-mile fun run and raised more than £200. A few days later she was dead but, wrote her husband, nothing would have deterred her because 'she felt so grateful for all the comfort and strength BACUP had given us, that she wanted to give whatever she could in return.'

Helen was a young woman who had had leukaemia and been helped by BACUP. She turned again to the organization where her father was diagnosed terminally ill with lung cancer. She and her parents talked frequently to the BACUP nurses during the last month of his life and her mother continued to ring one of the nurses after his death whenever she felt low. Helen felt she must do something in return and was offered a training as one of BACUP's volunteer counsellors. Doing this gave her the personal satisfaction of feeling that she was doing something useful and it also helped her to get over her father's death.

A young woman who had an operation on her foot for a malignant melanoma had been given no forewarning about the extent of her disfigurement. 'I felt stunned and deeply depressed – as though I had no control over what was happening to me.' By chance she saw a BACUP poster in her GP's surgery so she telephoned when she got home. The nurse was understanding and informative and immediately followed up the call with a leaflet. She could not bear to read it but her partner did and 'discovered there was hope for me after all. Once I had that information, I felt in control and confident in my ability to cope.' She later had a baby.

Occasionally an irate doctor would telephone and ask what BACUP thought it was doing, 'interfering' with one of his patients or something similar, but on the whole more doctors all the time were coming to see the value of the organization. They were willing to display the BACUP posters and distribute leaflets. It was all happening at last.

Vicky managed a fortnight's holiday in Jersey with David and Tim. In September Jennifer Butcher took up her post as fund-raiser for BACUP. Vicky had been present at her interview three months earlier but she was very silent and looked so ill that Jennifer was certain she would be dead before she arrived.

'I was willing her to live because I wanted to have the experience of working with her. It was wonderful to find her still there.'

Vicky swiftly established a good relationship with Jennifer who would visit her regularly in hospital as a way of keeping her in touch with what was going on. Jennifer recognized the star quality in Vicky and saw what a remarkable asset she had in the founder as a means of marketing the organization, provided that Vicky could stand the pace. Jennifer's conviction coincided with Vicky's realization that her best efforts for BACUP now lay in promoting it at every conceivable opportunity.

Not everyone would have agreed that a frail, moribund woman was the right person to be promoting anything, let alone an organization one of whose main aims was to inform and support cancer patients and encourage them to believe that it is possible to live positively with cancer. Vicky, however, was not a typical invalid. She was endowed with a quite remarkable degree of 'fighting spirit', a quality which cancer doctors recognize with awe. It can enable those patients who possess it to achieve extraordinary goals and successes at a time when everyone around them has more or less given up hope.

'Positive denial', another quality already mentioned, can be equally powerful: the patient has, at one level of consciousness, accepted the reality of their cancer and, then quite deliberately, pushes it away from the centre of their mind so that they can get on with the present, the job of living each day as it comes, to the full. Vicky achieved this superbly well. Of course, she knew she had incurable cancer and that, eventually, there would be no escape, she would die from it. She had never flinched from recognizing this fact and she had discussed the prospect of death many times at an early stage with her closest friends. Now that death had come so much closer and she had hung over the brink so often, she saw no reason to waste any of her precious time talking about its inevitability.

Vicky loved the limelight and being the centre of attention; this was another of her father's characteristics appearing belatedly, although no doubt it was helped by the cancer which gave her the excuse to be open about something she had possibly always yearned for in secret. One of her friends observed that, however ill Vicky might have been minutes earlier, the moment she was under the television lights or facing a microphone she seemed to absorb energy like an expanding flower. Jennifer, instead of disapproving of Vicky's self-centredness as some did, understood her need to be recognized.

'She was, after all, investing everything of herself in BACUP. It was natural for her to want to see something back. Otherwise she might just as well have concentrated on looking after herself.'

All the same, Jennifer, and others in the organization, were acutely aware of the danger that BACUP could be accused of exploiting Vicky's plight in a somewhat mawkish way to raise funds. It was a fine line to tread but the central player was a very skilled performer. What clinched it was her utter and completely genuine lack of self-pity. Vicky did not have an ounce of it. She never complained about her cancer, or even talked about it, except of course to those caring for her; or when it was for a good reason like explaining to medical students what it felt like to be a cancer patient. Although everyone who met her at this time knew she must be very ill, few people realized quite how far down the road she had already gone.

Very soon the honours and attention came pouring in thick and fast. In October 1986 Vicky was a special guest of honour at the Woman of the Year lunch, held annually at the Savoy. In the same month she was also awarded one of the nine Evian Health Awards for 1986; in her case for outstanding achievement in the campaign and promotions section and she received her award at a lunch in the Dorchester.

In November she managed to make the trip to Hong Kong although it was touch and go. Jennifer Butcher, who saw her the Friday night before the flight in her hospital bed, wired up to drips and hardly able to raise her head from the pillow, was certain it could not happen. On Monday Vicky telephoned her, sounding very perky, to inform her that she was safely ensconced in the Hong Kong Hilton. A special fridge had been installed for all her bags of food; she had travelled with a nurse and the room was fitted out like a mini-hospital.

One of Susie's friends who had known Vicky since she was a little girl, visited her there and recalls her shock at Vicky's emaciated appearance and amazement at her behaviour.

'She was just a shell and her room was full of medicines but she acted like there is no tomorrow. She just never talked about death or behaved like a dying person. She was buying shirts by the dozen and she was raving about the jewellery which she had been looking at in the Hilton shop.'

Vicky had a wonderful time. She was fêted and fussed over by her vast extended family – there were no less than sixty first cousins – and Auntie Winnie gave a grand lunch for all the aunts and uncles, including Stanley Ho. It was the week of the Macau Grand Prix and her father was president. It was his most favourite event of the year and he laid out the red carpet for his favourite daughter.

Vicky travelled across to Macau in a private hovercraft with a retinue of servants who wheeled her around the course and lifted her over the bridges in her wheelchair. She loved every moment of it. Back at the Hilton she received a constant stream of visitors and naturally, she found time to spread the message about BACUP, giving radio and press interviews.

On her return home she was immediately ill again with an infection and spent Christmas and the New Year in the Homerton Hospital. She managed to get out of her bed to attend Betty's wedding in February and then it was more see-sawing between hospital and home. She continued working for BACUP wherever she was and anyone involved with BACUP would receive letters from Vicky detailing BACUP's progress. They were dictated and signed by her and invariably personalized with a postscript. Any small job anyone did was also immediately acknowledged with a personal note. In March 1987 she sent out BACUP's first annual report which was called *Breaking the Silence on Cancer* and in her long accompanying letter Vicky pointed out that their annual estimated budget had now risen to £422,000 – a fourfold leap in less than two years.

April 1987 was a high spot in Vicky's calendar. She was elected to be a Fellow of her own college, the Royal College of Physicians, in recognition of her work at BACUP. On 13th April, the Monday of Easter week, she appeared on the *Wogan* show and was exceptionally good. The letters came pouring into BACUP immediately afterwards and Terry Wogan was so impressed by her courage and charm that he included her in his book of the most memorable people he has had on his show. She achieved this success despite the fact that she had great difficulty keeping her pain under control that day. The show had been pre-recorded on 9th April so that she could keep her promise to open BACUP's first contact point outside London. On 10th April she flew to Jersey for the official launch of Jersey BACUP, started by Celia Skinner, which took place on 14th April.

In May Vicky came from Homerton Hospital to pre-record her interview for the BBC television *Lifeline Appeal* which appeared on Sunday, 14th June. She was accompanied by Sister Jenny Ellwood who remembers a nightmare car drive, injecting Vicky at every traffic light with Buscopan for her abdominal pains while Vicky was rehearsing her speech. Once they arrived at Charterhouse Street Vicky lay on the sofa, drinking gallons of water and recovering her strength while the television crew prepared for filming. When they were ready, so was Vicky, with ten minutes of prepared text promoting BACUP. She was lucid and convincing, as good as ever. As soon as it was finished, she went back to the sofa where she slept for the rest of the afternoon.

This particular event had had its behind-the-scenes dilemma for BACUP. What if Vicky should die before the programme came out? Well, she did not and it was extremely successful, netting £34,000 for the charity. Although in hospital most of the time, whenever she could manage it she would escape from her bed to enjoy social events like the Chelsea Flower Show and Wimbledon, even though it meant lying on the floor of the hospitality tent for a good deal of the time.

June was another hectic month. There was the General Election on the 11th which meant that Tim was fully occupied. On the 12th and the 19th she did two long interviews with me. On Sunday, 14th June, the *Lifeline Appeal* which she had recorded a month earlier with Cliff Michelmore went out at six-fifteen in the evening. Vicky and David went into the studio to help answer the calls. On the 20th she went back to East Grinstead to her old school for a twenty-year reunion of her year. It was held in the original grammar school building and Vicky loved it. She was going back as a celebrity. On the 22nd June she did an interview on *Woman's Hour*; on the 24th she went to a charity cocktail party and on the 25th June she was presented to the Duchess of Kent at a Cancer Relief MacMillan Fund event.

On the night of 26th June Vicky took part in a television discussion called *After Dark* which went on from midnight into the small hours. The producer had agreed she need only stay on for one hour but in the end it lasted three hours with Vicky talking about cancer, death and BACUP. Tim who was waiting in the studio after a late meeting of the SDP National Executive was furious that she should be doing something so demanding in her weakened state. They had a row but late on Saturday afternoon they drove down to their cottage. Vicky pencilled a note in her diary: 'cottage & garden immaculate'.

She was very tired and in pain all that weekend. Her eyes were noticeably drooping. On Sunday evening, 28th June, Tim drove her straight to Barts where she was admitted into the Annie Zunz ward once more.

15

Good, Wasn't I?

❖

A MONTH LATER, on Thursday, 30th July 1987 at two-forty in the afternoon, Vicky Clement-Jones died, very peacefully, five years almost to the day that she had been diagnosed with cancer. Present were her husband Tim, her sister Betty, her friends, David, Alison and Michael, her doctor, Maurice Slevin, and Yvonne Terry from BACUP. She was in a side room off the Annie Zunz ward in St Bartholomew's Hospital. It was where she wanted to be when the end came, she had told David six months earlier. Tim and David were on either side of her, each holding one of her hands. She was still wearing a big watch Betty had given her – 'so she could always remain in control,' wrote Tim. When her breathing finally stopped, each person there said their private goodbye to her. Tim whispered: 'You really showed them.'

All long day people from the hospital and elsewhere had been dropping in just to say goodbye. Professor Tim McElwain had driven up from the Royal Marsden Hospital in Sutton. He stood at the door, silently looking at the small unconscious figure in the bed. Then he blew her a kiss and turned on his heel and drove back to Sutton. He never uttered a word.

Maurice Slevin had described the scene immediately follow-ing her death thus: 'As with her life, it was not a depressing time; that came later. There was a feeling of elation, a paradoxical high we all experienced as we stood and talked and joked about Vicky. To some this might sound disrespectful, cynical or even sick. It was not planned, it just happened. It was appropriate, it just felt right to everyone.'

Vicky had started that last month of her life with a diagnosis of myesthenia gravis, a muscular disorder which in her case was a side effect of overdosing on Buscopan. But, in her inimitable way, she started to revive. Indeed, so much better did she feel that she and Tim decided, after consulting Maurice, to book a holiday in Italy at the beginning of August. Maurice got clearance from the Home Office to enable them to take out sufficient morphine for her and they were both looking forward to it.

Vicky had trounced death so many times in the last year, surviving infections and dire complications of all kinds, that it had begun to seem perfectly reasonable to imagine she would succeed yet again. She had convinced Maurice to the extent that he even ordered twenty-four tubes of a special size for her gastrotomy (the drain in her stomach), enough to last six years as Vicky worked out on her calculator. But, she reminded him, it had taken six months to get these tubes so he must remember next time to order them at least one year in advance. She did not want to risk running out of them.

Madness? Sublime folly? The ultimate in self-deception? I would say none of these. Vicky did not so much lose touch with reality as put part of it to one side until she was ready to face it. She was not willing just to sit down and wait quietly for death. Neither, though, was it her way to 'go angry into that dark night'. She intended to live positively every conscious moment of her life until she died. That is exactly what she did.

Only on Wednesday, her last conscious day, when her powerful will could no longer control the effect of drugs so that she became distressingly restless, was she probably finally aware that this time she would not be coming back. Her last words to David that evening were a reassurance that whatever it looked like from the outside: 'it's calm inside here'.

To Sister Jo Hockley who had acquired a great admiration for Vicky over the months of nursing her, she had said earlier that day: 'Jo, it's so lovely. You have no idea.'

Vicky Clement-Jones died as she had lived, finding 'good in everything', even death.

Vicky's memorial service in St Paul's Cathedral on 3rd November 1987 was a triumphant celebration of her life and work. Hymns, music, poems and readings had all been carefully chosen by Tim and her close circle of friends. Colleagues and friends read the Lessons and gave the addresses. The Reverend Doug Hiza, the chaplain at the Homerton Hospital, gave the sermon.

It was a large gathering; probably more than one thousand people were there, all of whom were present because at some time in their lives Vicky had made a lasting impression on them. For many she had been a catalyst that had changed their lives. Janet Suzman, the actress, who had done a benefit for BACUP, when asked by a television reporter why she was attending the service, gave a simple and moving answer: 'Vicky Clement-Jones was one of Nature's great human beings.'

There were also some in that congregation who were probably reflecting to themselves with some wonderment, could it really be true? They were in that solemn place simply because they had been privileged to know Vicky? Who would have thought it?

Vicky for one would not have been at all surprised. She would have taken it as her due. The memorial service was her last party and, true to Vicky, it was in grand style. But it was not all pomp and circumstance.

Vicky herself was never a solemn person as Professor Tim

McElwain, in his eloquent address, reminded everyone. Nor, despite her remarkable achievements, was she 'a sort of medical Joan of Arc. In fact she was wonderfully funny, cheerful and down to earth. As well as having so many admirable characteristics she also had a host of endearing ones. For me, her most lovable characteristic was her total lack of false modesty, her certain knowledge that she was special.'

He then recounted a favourite story which he had witnessed and told on many other occasions:

'One day when she was walking across the meat market on the way to BACUP she was hailed by a porter. "Saw you on the box last night," he said. "Good, wasn't I?" she replied. Well, she was, wasn't she? She was good and clever and funny and creative and constant and brave and inspirational; and out of all that pain and suffering and uncertainty she brought forth BACUP and that is her memorial.'

Si monumentum requiris, circumspice (If you seek his monument, look round) is the inscription in St Paul's dedicated to its architect, Christopher Wren, by his son.

This majestic temple was a fitting place to be reminded that BACUP is Vicky's living memorial. It was a remarkable creation to have achieved in three short years, the more so when one considers that she was racked with pain and illness for all of that time. The work that Vicky did in that short period was so well done that she would know, already by the end of her life, that she had touched literally thousands of lives and that untold thousands more in the future would be the better for her efforts. Vicky, says Tim, always wanted to make a name for herself and leave something behind by which she would be remembered. Outstandingly gifted in many ways, Vicky made a special gift − BACUP − to her adopted country.

Professor McElwain called Vicky a star in his address. Her

old friend, Pamela, said that Vicky made stars of her friends. She was generous about bringing out their talents and if sometimes she played the puppet master she did it with such genuine affection that few grudged her the manipulation. Vicky was one of those life-enhancing people who can light up even the most dreary corners of life and when she came face to face with something so profoundly life-threatening as cancer she refused to allow it to extinguish her zest for life. Her enthusiasm was infectious and irresistible, not only for her friends but in the last years of her life for most people she met.

Vicky said more than once that her whole life had been a training for BACUP. Nature and nurture both had served to endow Vicky with all the attributes needed to create such an outstanding organization.

Vicky was remarkable in so many ways that it becomes difficult to write about her without sounding extravagant. Her life is statement enough. There is no doubt, however, that it was the circumstance of cancer which brought everything together and turned her into that rare phenomenon – a visionary who makes the dream come true. 'Anyone can have an idea; it's what you do with it that counts,' commented one of her colleagues, Professor Phil Lowry, to me.

It had taken two years for Vicky to crystallize the concept of BACUP – the idea that had first surfaced as 'I'm going to kick cancer out of the closet' – but once she had it, she was determined to see it through. Anyone who threatened that aim, even if it was only by well-meaning criticism, was anathema; they could even be considered an enemy. This explains why some people did find it difficult to work with Vicky. She could not tolerate dissent or any sign of lagging. It was so clear in her own mind what had to be done and how it had to be done, and all on such a reduced and uncertain time scale, that she became very impatient with people who appeared to be putting unnecessary spokes in the turning wheel.

Cancer freed Vicky. First it freed her from the need to compete and this was a surprising relief to her. She had not realized how weary she had become of the medical rat-race. And when the cancer recurred, Vicky had a second, more profound liberation. She realized that not only could she drop out of the race altogether but now she had been given a chance to concentrate on something much more worth while and fulfilling. In a sense she had won permission to concentrate all her formidable energies and intellect on something she really wanted to do, not what she thought she ought to do. When people used to ask her whether she would not prefer to spend more time on herself, she would respond quite simply and with total honesty: 'BACUP is my life. There's nothing else I want to spend my time on. How many people do you know who have been lucky enough to see their dream come true?'

Cancer empowered Vicky. It gave her opportunities which again she did not hesitate to seize. Her early fears that she might use her illness to manipulate people quickly evaporated when she had a cause to promote rather than herself. She never asked for sympathy for herself but she could talk so compellingly about the needs that BACUP was serving that people who might otherwise have tried to escape were shamed into giving whatever she asked for. She exulted in her power and became, as David used to tell her, 'a shameless hussy' in her deployment of it, but it was always in the cause of BACUP. There was no guile in Vicky.

Cancer enriched Vicky. It put her in touch with a vast circle of people who might otherwise never have crossed her path. She learnt many new skills and she discovered new talents in herself. She learnt much more about herself and she gained insights into other people's lives and motivation. Cancer deepened her own humanity and made her a more understanding and compassionate person. It gave her the time to say the things she wanted to say to those closest to her and it gave her the opportunity to do the things she might otherwise have put off doing. Above all cancer gave her the sense of purpose she always knew she had been seeking but had not been certain where to look. Cancer gave meaning to her life.

Cancer emboldened and developed her own personality. She became charismatic. Although she had always been abundantly energetic and enthusiastic, she had also been quite a quiet person. Not a mouse exactly but not a tiger either. Indeed Tim used to get angry with her because she was so bad at fighting her own battles. Once, however, Vicky had become identified as BACUP, nothing and no one fazed her. Cancer gave her permission to break rules and initiate new ventures. If she thought something was worth pursuing for the advancement of BACUP, nothing could stop her. She loved meeting the great, the good and the famous and she lapped up the adulation and compliments that came her way. Centre stage was where Vicky liked to be and now she did not have to pretend any more. The little girl who had once sought attention and love and recognition so desperately, now had it heaped upon her unstintingly.

Vicky was no saint. She was certainly not a model of meek resignation and she could be difficult and demanding. She could also be single-minded to the point of ruthlessness in pursuit of her own goals. She was not a back-stabber or a hand-stamper but she had no time to waste, or pity to spare for people she felt were not as committed and wholeheartedly in pursuit of the cause as she was. No one would ever describe Vicky as sweet and a lot of people would say they admired her rather than that they liked her. She inspired strong emotions and, no doubt, if she had lived would have become something of a despot. She was capable of treating people quite disdainfully, especially those who were doing a service for her. Her close family who looked after her devotedly were often ignored and disregarded.

Vicky frequently talked about the importance of the family to the cancer patient. She did not always acknowledge her family's generosity towards her but inwardly she knew that she could not have achieved all that she did without the unstinting and unconditional love they gave her. She would never have lived so long without the care and devotion that she received from Tim, her husband, and David, her dearest friend. That is why she felt it was so important for the relatives and friends of cancer to feel that BACUP was an organization for them too.

There were many people, especially those who loved 'Vicks', who felt sad, even angry on her behalf, that despite the brilliant pack of cards she had been shuffled, in the end she was dealt a rotten hand. It did not seem fair to have that lethal card turning up so early in her life.

Vicky never felt that way. All her life she had thrived on meeting challenges and winning races. Cancer was the biggest challenge to come into her life and Vicky was determined to bust it. Since eventually she had to come to terms with the fact that she would not be able to beat the cancer in herself, this made her all the more determined to defeat the destructive attitudes and behaviour so often induced by this disease.

'Knowledge is the antidote to fear,' she used to say. Through BACUP she brought knowledge and understanding to many people. Cancer patients and their families and friends are the major beneficiaries of Vicky's work. To quote Tim McElwain again: 'She gave them back their dignity and sense of importance; she handed back to them control over their lives; she helped them to feel valued.'

Vicky's ripple effect goes wider even than that. She has also had a profound effect on the behaviour and attitudes of the health professionals. The doctors and nurses who looked after her were inspired by her example and her courage as she dealt with each new devastating onslaught. Many of them told me how much they had learnt from Vicky's management of her disease. The existence of BACUP and the proof of its worth has meant that doctors and nurses everywhere are beginning to lose their own fear of cancer. Honest, open communication, which Vicky regarded as absolutely vital in the patient-doctor relationship, is slowly being accepted as something that not only can be quite easily effected but should always be there as part of the treatment.

Vicky has been proved triumphantly right. If you search hard enough and have the will to do something positive, it is possible to find good in everything, even cancer. Many cancer patients will identify with the discoveries that Vicky made about herself and for others.

16

BACUP is Sailing

❖

M ANY A TIME Doug Hiza had said goodbye to Vicky on a Friday afternoon in her side room off the Gordon Hamilton-Fairley ward in Hackney and wondered whether he would see her again the following Monday. In almost thirty years of ministry he said he had never seen such a strong will to live as that shown by Vicky. It was certainly not the medication which was keeping her alive but, whatever it was, it was not verbalized. They would talk of many other things but sometimes when she seemed to have moved on to a different spiritual plane he would just sit silently in the room with her, saying prayers for her.

Alison can remember that when Vicky was really ill she would turn her face to the wall and concentrate all her energies on staying alive just getting through the episode, however terrible it might be. Vicky was determined not to let go before she was ready. The power of her will was palpable. 'You could walk into the room and feel it,' said Alison.

Sometime during her last month of life Vicky probably felt released from that need to hang on to life. One day she said to Jo Hockley: 'It's all right. I do feel that BACUP is sailing.'

For so long and against overwhelming odds Vicky had dedicated everything of herself to the creation and development of BACUP. She had set the ship on course, fixed the compass and trained the crew. Now the time had come for her to hand over the wheel. She could do so in the sure knowledge that those who took over from her would carry on the work as she had begun it. BACUP was her legacy and her proof to posterity that the presence of Vicky in the world had made a significant difference to the lives of many people. Furthermore, it was certain now that her influence would ripple on long after her death.

The one preparation Vicky never made was to lay precise plans for her succession. In all those long hours of discussing BACUP with Maurice Slevin she never once alluded to a future when she would not be there nor did she suggest, by even the merest hint, that she would like him to take over as Chairman. It could be said that it was unnecessary to make explicit a wish which had been so clearly implicit ever since she had contrived his election as her deputy Chairman. It was undoubtedly more than even brave Vicky could bear to do: think about it, yes, but not actually talk about the time when she would no longer be present to direct BACUP, her precious dream come true.

Just as she had secured Maurice, whom she could trust to be faithful to her wishes because he believed so strongly in the ideal of BACUP and they had worked together so closely every step of the way, so she made doubly sure that there could be no deviation by asking the Executive to agree that Tim, her most loyal supporter, should become one of the Trustees. This she effected back in February 1986 when she thought she was going to die. Vicky had never liked the idea of a family charity but she knew that BACUP would be in safe hands if Tim was put in a strong position to remind everyone, should they ever be tempted to forget, what she would have wanted.

Vicky never talked directly about her own death to any but those closest to her. To people she did not know very well she tended to speak in circumlocutions, probably to spare herself as much as them from embarrassment or a feeling that they might have to make some conventional expression of regret. Thus, if she were discussing some plan or intention for BACUP that might take a while to realize she would say, 'If I'm run over by a bus you must do . . .' or, if someone asked her how it felt to live in the shadow of death, she would duck away with a phrase like: 'If you're asking me whether I think I'll collect my old-age pension, I have to say no.' I have been surprised by the annoyance that so many people felt about this. 'Vicky was into denial,' they say as if this was a reprehensible state of mind. But why should she talk to all and sundry about her innermost feelings regarding the most important life-event that faces each one of us? Vicky had confronted the beast a long time ago and had made her own pact with it. Now she was going to live every day fully until the final moment of surrender.

Undoubtedly, it is difficult to live in close proximity to a dying person whose continued existence in defiance of all the prognoses can be seen as something of a reproach. Vicky's incredible will to live and her refusal to admit defeat somehow also manage to serve as a constant reminder to everyone around her of their own inescapable mortality. These are difficult emotions to live with because on the whole most of us survive by pushing the unthinkable right away into the darkest corner of our mind.

For the last eighteen months of her life Vicky was not really directing BACUP. She was physically incapable of doing anything beyond her brilliant promotion of the organization so she depended on the Trustees, the deputy Chairman and the Executive to supervise the managers and, eventually, make the policy decisions. However, she refused to let go entirely and this did cause problems for the staff at BACUP. They lived, as one of them said with great feeling, 'in a state of endless uncertainty'. Some people who joined the organization towards the end of her life hardly knew Vicky. When she did manage a visit to the offices, she tended to talk to the nurses, rather forgetting that without the backup and resources supplied by the other members of staff the Cancer Information Service could not have functioned as well as it did. People were torn between feeling pity for Vicky and, at other times, frustration when they longed to order things differently but felt that they could not oppose someone who was so near death. Vicky was not unaware of the power her illness gave her nor did she scruple to use that power if she felt it was to the advantage of BACUP.

Although everyone at BACUP knew that one day fairly soon Vicky would no longer be there, when she did die the shock was profound. The anticipation of loss bore no resemblance to the reality. Their charismatic leader had left them and there is no doubt that for a while there was an underlying sense of panic that they might not be able to carry on.

BACUP has always been a youthful organization, cast in the image of its founder; for most members of staff Vicky's death was their first major bereavement. Those who had been close to her had to cope with their grief while carrying on with their job. Others might have felt more detached but they still had to cope with the unhappiness of their mourning colleagues. The ship juddered and creaked as it plunged through some very heavy seas. Inevitably and sadly, as always happens in times of change and development, there were upheavals and departures. Meanwhile the work had to go on. The calls continued to come in; the need for the service became, if anything, even more evident. The belief that what they were doing was important and valued was probably what saved the crew from disaster. Eventually the ship – so solidly built – righted itself and proceeded on the course Vicky had prepared for it so carefully and with such vision.

BACUP has entered the last decade of the century running swiftly and confidently before the wind of change under the assured guidance of its Chairman, Dr Maurice Slevin, and the able management of its Director, Olivia Dix, appointed in 1988. The Executive, led by three Trustees who include Tim Clement-Jones, continues to meet regularly and to exercise a supervisory and policy-framing role. The early suspicion that BACUP's sudden arrival and meteoric progress aroused in some of the other cancer support organizations has dissolved as they have been able to observe and appreciate the unique contribution it offers to the welfare of cancer patients and their families and friends.

By November 1990, five years after its inception, the Cancer Information Service had responded to more than 100,000 enquiries; in 1990, the last full year for figures, this represented an average of just over eighty telephone calls a day. Nearly forty per cent of these enquiries are from friends and relatives; thirty per cent are from patients; and the rest are from health professionals (eleven per cent), support groups and the general public. The enquirers are predominantly female (more than eighty per cent) and the cancer most commonly asked about is breast cancer.

A freeline has been established for callers from outside London and every call is recorded on a detailed form (now in its fourteenth version), which provides a rich data base of information for computerization and evaluation. BACUP will use it to plan the future expansion of the service and hopes that other organizations and research centres will also take advantage of this resource. More than 100,000 leaflets and booklets are sent out free of charge by first-class post to enquirers every year.

'It was marvellous to receive all your information the next day,' wrote one grateful client. 'It made me feel you really cared.'

This is a sentiment repeated by many, so much so that BACUP regards it as a top priority to establish the lines of communication as quickly as possible. During a recent period of financial stringency when the Executive had to consider cuts, the proposal that the postage should be made second class was turned down by a resounding majority.

The service is run on a daily office hours basis by the equivalent of ten full-time nurses, each one of whom spends no more than half a day at a time on the telephone. This is quite long enough, given the harrowing nature of many of the calls, and avoids burn-out, a hazard suffered by many of the first nurses. The other half of the day is spent on writing letters, working on a relevant project, giving talks about BACUP and receiving information updates from medical specialists.

The BACUP Cancer Counselling Service, using trained volunteers, took some time to establish but it is now growing rapidly and currently holds seventy-eight sessions a month. The volunteer counsellors (who do not have to have had cancer but should have some personal experience of what it means) are carefully selected and trained. Linda Benn, the present manager, hopes to extend the service into the regions as soon as she has enough trained counsellors and supervisors. Eventually, she envisages that BACUP will be providing a model of excellence for cancer counselling, similar to that provided by the Samaritans for the suicidal and the Cruse organization for the bereaved.

All this needs money and BACUP never has enough to meet all the demands that are made on it. It employs twenty-five full-time staff and a varying number of freelance nurses. Its annual expenditure is now close to £1 million, one fifth of which comes from the major cancer charities and the remainder is raised entirely from voluntary donations ranging from big City corporations, trusts, local groups and the like, to individual cheques from grateful individuals. It receives minimal government funding (£11,000) even though several MPs have made appeals on its behalf, most notably the Liberal MP Simon Hughes in a House of Commons Debate on cancer on 13th March 1987.

He made a strong recommendation to the then Minister of Health, Edwina Currie, that BACUP deserved reliable and adequate public funding since it was responsible for giving comfort and support to so many distressed people, Cancer, after all, affects one in three of the population.

Plans for the future include a regional network to act as a focus for information delivery and fund-raising purposes; a patient to patient volunteer service; and an extended educational role, taking full advantage of BACUP's expanding and possibly unique library resource. The first two aims were clearly expounded at Vicky's first Working Party Meeting and the third, though not precisely formulated by her, is absolutely consistent with the importance she placed on communication.

'BACUP provides a place of safety for a frightened person. Essentially, it puts people who want to talk in touch with people who want to listen,' said someone who worked at BACUP in its early years. She offered her services to the organization because she was so impressed by Vicky when she met her at one of the hospital cancer support groups that she attended so assiduously in the early days of her illness.

The Reverend Doug Hiza described Vicky as a teacher, a pioneer and a pilgrim in his sermon at her Memorial Service. BACUP, the 'rather grand dream' she had once dared to dream and lived long enough to see come entirely true, embodies all these elements within its present framework.

BACUP (British Association of Cancer United Patients)

121 Charterhouse Street, London EC 1

Cancer Information Service (tel: 071-608-1661)

Freeline 0800 181199 (outside London)

Counselling Service (tel: 071-608-1038)
